A Handbook of Common Groupwork Problems

A Handbook of Common Groupwork Problems tackles issues and problems encountered by groupworkers in everyday practice. Tom Douglas has worked with, taught, and acted as consultant to groups and groupworkers for many years, and has distilled this wide-ranging experience into a practical self-help programme for groupworkers.

Based on the most common problems Dr Douglas has been consulted about during the last twenty years, the *Handbook* highlights how practical problems remain remarkably similar for every new generation of workers. It proposes a method for analysing common problems, showing how to break down the analysis into target areas, and to devise, put into action, and monitor strategies to deal with these problems. The focus is on five broad areas – the members of a group; the group as a system; the conditions which affect a group; leadership roles; and the supervision, training and development of groupworkers. There is also much practical advice on how to use known resources and develop potential ones within the group.

This essentially practical approach will be specially helpful to groupworkers without access to supervision or consultation, and makes the *Handbook* an immensely valuable resource and effective training guide for all who work with or in groups.

A Handbook of Common Groupwork Problems

Tom Douglas

Tavistock/Routledge
London and New York

First published in 1991
by Routledge
11 New Fetter Lane, London EC4P 4EE

Simultaneously published in the USA and Canada
by Routledge
a division of Routledge, Chapman and Hall, Inc.
29 West 35th Street, New York, NY 10001

Printed and bound in Great Britain by Mackays of Chatham PLC, Kent

British Library Cataloguing in Publication Data
Douglas, Tom
  A Handbook of Common Groupwork Problems.
  1. Welfare work: Groupwork
  I. Title
  361.4

Library of Congress Cataloging in Publication Data
Douglas, Tom.
  A Handbook of Common Groupwork Problems/Tom Douglas.
  p. cm.
  Includes bibliographical references and index.
  1. Group psychotherapy. 2. Small groups – Psychological aspects.
  I. Title.
  RC488.D68 1991   90–46814
  616.89'152 – dc20   CIP

ISBN 0–415–03897–9
     0–415–03898–7 (pbk)

To the memory of my brother George Douglas

Contents

Acknowledgements   ix

Part I Introduction

1 Introduction – sources and structure   3
   The reasons for compiling a handbook of common
       groupwork problems   3
   The sources of material used in this book   6
   Discussion of the common problems which emerge
       and of some interesting omissions   8
   The nature of problems in groups   10
   The pattern of presentation and the effective methods
       of using this book   14
   The relationship of an analysis of common problems
       to the development of groupwork skill   16
   Strategies: their nature and use   18

Part II Common groupwork problems

2 An explanation of the classification system   25
3 Problems relating to the members of a group   28
4 Problems relating to the group as a system   85
5 Problems relating to the conditions that affect the
   group   112
6 Problems relating to the performance of leadership
   roles   140
7 Problems relating to the supervision, training and
   development of groupworkers   165

Part III Discussion

8 Summing up   183
  Some reiteration of methods of using this handbook   183
  Other strategies available for problem resolution and
     management   184
  What happens when strategies do not work?   185
  Summing up   186

Index   189

Acknowledgements

I owe a great debt to all those who, collectively and individually over the years, have shared with me their successes and their problems in many fields of groupwork. They are far too numerous to mention here but they include colleagues and students; the members of many courses, workshops, and seminars. In particular I would mention the Groupwork Network of Nottingham; the Family Placement Groupworkers of Cheshire; the Community Mental Handicap Team Workshops held under the aegis of the British Institute of Mental Handicap; workshops at the Universities of Keele and Queen's, Belfast. I hope that all those who participated in these events will think that their efforts in discussing their work have been worthwhile.

As usual I have received unflagging support and encouragement from my wife Shirley who has devoted much time to reading the draft manuscript.

Part I

Introduction

Chapter 1

Introduction – sources and structure

THE REASONS FOR COMPILING A HANDBOOK OF COMMON GROUPWORK PROBLEMS

In 1961 a paper by Bradford, Stock and Horwitz appeared in the National Training Laboratory Institute Selected Reading Series, vol. 1 (Group development) entitled, 'How to diagnose group problems'. It was a remarkable article in that it concentrated on what was defined as the 'three most common group problems', which were (1) conflict or fight, (2) apathy and non-participation and (3) inadequate decision-making, and gave quite a lengthy list of symptoms of these problems and their possible causes. Moreover the paper went on to indicate that a three-part process, that is, collecting information, reporting information to the group and making diagnoses and decisions for change, was an appropriate way of tackling these problems.

This paper has remained relatively unique in groupwork literature in that it is not concerned with the setting in which groupwork is practised, nor in the underlying theory, nor with a particular client population, nor with starting or stopping a group, which are all the usual diet of groupwork literature, but with those factors which commonly adversely affect the running efficiency of any group.

Indeed the paper begins with this statement:

> A group has two things in common with a machine or with any organism anywhere: 1. It has something to do. 2. It must be kept in running order to do it.
>
> (Bradford, Stock and Horwitz 1961: 37)

The analogy with a machine is not exact, but the authors use it tellingly to insist that a group must be maintained in good working order by the removal or modification of those factors which would, if left to themselves, impair its functional efficiency.

For me this paper constituted what I would call a 'milestone' paper in that it opened up a very simple and obvious 'need-to-know'. If a group is created or adapted to perform certain beneficial functions then it goes without saying that it will be required to be kept in the best possible condition in order to do its job. Which leads me to state what I consider to be the two major deficiencies of this otherwise excellent paper:

1 It is based upon theoretical concepts and the individual experience of the authors.
2 It omits the problems of recognition.

I will deal briefly with these points here as they will occur much more specifically later in the text and in greater detail.

Over quite a long period of time I have become aware of a discrepancy between the material which is taught to groupworkers, what is presented to them in textbooks, and the kind of questions to which they seek to gain answers in workshops and in discussion. Essentially the latter are presented as practical difficulties and frustrations, and because practice wisdom is not so readily available to most practitioners and because the connection between a personal practical problem involved in working with a particular group and the literature, which might be presumed to exist to cope with just such exigencies, is seldom obvious, people are left often enough with the complex task of trying to work out a resolution from their own resources.

Now while this independence may be laudable in some ways, it also tends to be very wasteful of scarce resources in that by far the greater part of the difficulties groupworkers encounter as individuals for the first time have been met with previously elsewhere, and some kind of coping strategy worked out, some good, some not so good.

All problems which occur in group are in one sense unique to that group because of the unique nature of the group's members, its setting, and so on. But we have learned that the underlying processes of group behaviour, the patterns formed at some larger level than the idiosyncrasies of individual behaviour, create for our discovery a remarkable degree of similarity in all group forms. Indeed, were this not so, then the numerous attempts made over the last half century to formulate systematic programmes of group development would have been mere conceit. But we know that there is ample evidence that wholly independent definitions of the progress of a group, independent that is of professional manipulation, have demonstrated a degree of coincidence with the accepted paradigms which is many times greater than could ever have been expected by chance. Wholly unsophisticated group observers are quite capable of seeing and of charting group development with a very close approximation to the stages defined by researchers. The terminology may be somewhat different but this is to be expected.

So we must accept that, for whatever reason, there are 'regularities' there to be seen (see Chapter 4 on the concept of group structures). Thus there is knowledge already available about most forms of group behaviour. The problems seem to be twofold: first, in gaining access to it, and second, in discovering what is relevant to current need. There may well be a third difficulty which resides in the fact that most written material tends to be so specific, for example, a record of a single instance, or so large, for example, at the level of a general theory, that drawing from it sustenance to make a plan of action requires a very special skill which few teach and most learn, if they do, from sheer necessity. The questions practitioners ask have, from time to time, a very familiar ring to them, which draws me to make two inexorable inferences. First, that people working with and in teams and groups face problems which as far as group maintenance is concerned are relatively few in number, but occur and recur in almost every instance and for every generation. Second, a different slant on the same issue is the fact that in the time I have been working with groups, that is, since the early 1950s, the nature of these problems has changed little if at all.

It is not that I would not expect groups set up or taken over to achieve specific beneficial ends to throw up the same kind of problems because, obviously, the regularities which were referred to earlier would see to that. What does concern me is that each wave of groupworkers, generation by generation, seem to find themselves ill equipped to deal with the same problems despite an enormous increase in teaching and interest over the last thirty years.

It has long been my contention that the only wholly satisfactory method of acquiring skill in working with groups is a form of apprenticeship to a skilled and experienced groupworker/teacher; a method which combines the necessity to understand the available theories of group behaviour but which creates the bridge necessary to translate this into a personal method of working through intensely supervised practice. Out of this grows not just a practice skill as defined by a series of techniques, but also a personal method for the recognition of difficulties and of the ability to have sufficient basic schema to deal with even those problems which have never been met with before purely on the analysis of their fundamental rather than their superficial nature. Not least amongst the habits that may well develop in this process will be that kind of relationship with one's teacher/supervisor which is in essence truly consultative.

Perhaps the lack of general availability of the method which I have just outlined is at the root of the apparent lack of ability of groupworkers and of group-interested people noted earlier to cope with the similar problems of groupwork which have been appearing over such a long period of time. As we have all at some time or other discovered to our chagrin, there is no certain connection between a highly-developed theoretical knowledge of group behaviour and high levels of practical skill in work with groups composed of 'real' people. Equally it is true that skill developed without a complex understanding of those same group-behaviour theoretical concepts will, while no doubt possessing considerable flair, tend to remain limited in focus and constrained in development and will often perpetuate essentially simple errors for lack of a true understanding of their cause. That a system of apprenticeship will never develop except in certain favoured institutions is a fact of life. This handbook is an attempt to present a point of reference to all those who are excluded wholly or partially from such an ideal system. It seeks to make positive what has usually been seen as negative, namely the limited number of common problems and the frequency of their occurrence; to state them clearly in a manner based upon an analysis of the problems offered to me over the years by practitioners; to give examples, so that others can recognize similarities with issues that concern them; to look at possible causes; to offer what have been proven to be effective ways of designing strategies to meet these needs in the past; to indicate how the application of a strategy can be monitored, and how a feedback loop can be created and sustained; and finally to offer at least some material from the literature which may be useful.

Any book is but an inferior way of attempting to develop a practical skill, but flow charts have a record of success in improving and in nurturing very basic practical abilities and at least a handbook can form the basis of a guide to effective principles. Working in and with groups and teams successfully is such a complex human behaviour that no 'wiring' chart or set of charts can possibly cope with it. But I hope that the guide lines provided here will show the basic principles which underlie all strategies and allow practitioners to channel their energy and commitment into a series of appropriate responses.

THE SOURCES OF MATERIAL USED IN THIS BOOK

The importance of the maintenance function is immediately recognized in other situations. Airlines require the service of maintenance crews as well as navigators. An automobile, a sewing machine, a typewriter, or a whirling peanut wagon that has no care paid to its upkeep soon begins to break down.

(Bradford, Stock and Horwitz 1961:37)

Continuing the analogy of maintaining the functional efficiency of an operating system it would seem logical that the knowledge of what usually goes wrong with that system should be found mainly in the experience of those within it. This is not wholly true as any mechanic will confirm, in that although operators may be aware that something has gone wrong, unless they have some of the mechanic's skill and knowledge they cannot be precise about its cause. But at least they have good reason to know that something is preventing the system from performing efficiently. I have already indicated briefly the sources of the problems used in this book, but I feel that some information about the nature of the resulting selection would be appropriate here.

There are two main sources of problem material:

1 Written material presented by those who have attended workshops concerned with some aspect of group or team-work or who have written directly to me, often as a result of such workshops, and
2 problems which have been delivered verbally in many different group situa-

tions and which I have recorded for their 'value' to me and my colleagues in providing a focus for learning.

At this point it would seem appropriate to mention that the strategies which will be offered and discussed here also stem from two major sources, namely:

1 From the discussions which took place in group workshops and other situations where we attempted to define the real nature of the problems with which we were concerned and to go on to devise and try out action plans designed to deal with part, usually a significant but attainable part, of the problem if the whole issue proved unamenable.
2 The cumulative wisdom which is available in the large and growing literature on working with groups and teams throughout the world, augmented by and refined by discussion and consultation with groupworkers at all levels of practice.

I think that it is necessary here to state as clearly as possible, that if the reader can find here no reference to a particular groupwork problem which he/she may consider to be a serious oversight, then that omission is due to one solitary fact – that it has never been presented to me in all the time that I have been listening to groupworkers. Or, if it has, it has been offered so infrequently that it could by no stretch of the imagination be called 'common'. There may be several reasons for this which will, I think, bear a brief stating. They are:

(a) I have chosen to deal with problems which I have labelled 'common' in the belief, stated earlier, that the frequency of their presentation must indicate that to offer some help with these particular problems would reach a large audience of interested workers and provide some assistance in moving their groupwork practice forward.
(b) Some probably very significant and frustrating problems may not be all that 'common', relating clearly to very specific or unique issues.
(c) I am certain that although I have worked with and met groupworkers from many fields of endeavour and heard some of their problems, it would be manifestly impossible in one short life to have talked with people from all aspects of groupwork.
(d) There may be an element of what is fashionable in the kind of problems which are presented – though I doubt that this is a great selector.
(e) People tend to present problems to those they think may be sympathetic to them and their kind of work. I know that I am 'not everyone's cup of tea'[1] as one reviewer described me recently, and it is thus highly probable that a selective bias has entered in in this way based on the preferences of some practitioners.

There is another aspect of this which I propose to discuss in the next section. It is concerned with the fact that given all the reasons listed above for selective bias, there are still some interesting and puzzling gaps in the material, which do not seem attributable to anything so far covered.

DISCUSSION OF THE COMMON PROBLEMS WHICH EMERGE
AND OF SOME INTERESTING OMISSIONS

As I have indicated earlier, 'common' equals 'most often presented', and I have commented on the possible sources of bias in that presentation. But having said this there are some omissions which still cannot be fairly accounted for in this way and which may have something to do with fundamental and probably inflexible assumptions on the part of groupworkers.

For instance, I believe that groupwork is held by its practitioners to have such a universality and flexibility that the members of all cultures, races and societies are equally at home with it. It is interesting to note that one of the main problem areas explored later is how groupworkers can handle the problems which they see as arising from the 'difference' or 'diversity' of their group members. It is also interesting that similarity of problem or of need is by far the greatest single factor in the selection of potential group members. Difference, it is usually assumed, will only serve to shed new light on old problems, and in many instances this is true. But when the differences considered contain a very different upbringing, culture, religion and set of attitudes, then, unless steps are taken to recognize the possible effects of these differences, they can become more important than all the common problems that all may face.

Why do we find that in order to feel that they are certain of being understood in group situations, some of our ethnic minorities feel compelled to form groups which have similarity of race, background and culture as a fundamental necessity? Is it the same factor which helps to create self-help groups – that of an understanding which is obtained by the actual experience of being? It is a fact that in the selection of problems considered here those associated with member difference/diversity seldom are openly explicit except in the factors of social class, social competence and probably intelligence and certainly chronological age.

Another interesting point which emerges from these 'common problems' is the scant reference to theoretical knowledge. What appears to be the most common reference to such knowledge in verbal exchanges with practitioners takes the form of either 'My course was very interesting, but does not seem now to have much relevance to the work I am trying to do with groups' (this is a direct comment on the exposure to group behaviour theory on training courses) or, 'Being a member of a training group as a student was a good/bad experience and may have done much/little for me as a person, but did not really equip me for the job of working with groups in my work situation'.

Obviously these are composite statements, paraphrases, containing the essence of what has been said by many people in part over a long period of time. The most important piece of information presented in this context always seems to me to be about supervised practice. If a student's supervisor has worked out an effective *modus operandi* – then given the fact that the student is compatible with that way of working, the development in individual groupwork skill seems assured. However, more of this later in the section on problems arising from supervision, training and development.

One factor which I find quite astounding, revealed by the way in which certain kinds of problems are stated, is the factor of *time*. It is almost inconceivable that groupworkers should be so unaware of the time which is essential for certain things to happen. It is no accident that accelerators, devices designed to expedite the development of trust between group members in the early stages of the group or to erect structural patterns which facilitate working together in a well-defined area, have proliferated. The fact that they are often badly used may be credited to the acceptance of them as useful tools without any credible understanding of the bases upon which they rest. But, nevertheless, their use points either to an impatience to be done with the formative stages or a perception that in reality the time available is not sufficient to allow the group to develop at its own pace. The latter is perhaps a polite way of indicating that expectations are solidly based in a lack of real knowledge of time.

Of course some groups have reasons for existence which can be met and their aims accomplished without much attempt at creating a cohesive group being either necessary or desirable. Thus the word 'appropriate' once more has to be stressed. The time necessary to develop a group to perform a particular function should be calculated on the basis of what has been found to be appropriate in the many similar situations which have been recorded. Why is it that administrators accept the appropriateness of a multi-disciplinary team and yet seldom set aside sufficient time for its proper creation? This lack of understanding creates underfunctioning and sometimes self-destroying teams who may well believe that their poor performance reflects upon their competence. It more properly rests with the lack of understanding of the very long period of time necessary for members, all of high status, to work out their appropriate amount of commitment to the group and to create a structure in which the resources available to the group can be used. After all, a group possesses no energy other than that which is contributed by its members, and because a unit has been organizationally created and called a 'team' it does not mean that it is even minimally functionally effective unless that energy and those resources have been willingly and knowingly committed.

Another point to make is the apparent lack of problems relating to the large patterns of group performance – the so-called 'group processes'. This is indicated by the individual nature of most of the comments. It would seem that after years of exposure to the dynamics of groups the least common form of thinking of those who work with and in groups is (with apologies to Orwell) 'groupthink', that is, the ability to see the group as a single functioning unit in which its members, highly complex human beings though they are, are but its component and energizing parts.

Three other omissions from the offered material emerge quite clearly – termination, transformation and concern about why we use groups in the first place. The first is a major omission, the second has hardly ever begun to be considered and the third may mean that those who ask the questions have never seriously doubted that they should work with groups.

It is interesting to note that there is a great deal of material concerned with the process of starting a group and although most of the literature gives some consideration to stopping one, practitioners seem to see no problems in achieving this. There are several possible reasons, for instance:

1 It could be that most groups are 'open' and thus in a very real sense ever-lasting – so termination relates to individuals leaving and not to the group as a whole.
2 It could be that termination of those 'closed' groups which are formed is seen as 'natural' – a process which occurs in the same way that living things die whether preparation is made for the event or not.
3 It could be that groups effect a 'transformation' from one state to another by changing one or more of their structural components, for example, a reduction in the frequency of meetings; the adoption of new and different rules, goals, and so on. Many groups do 'transform' almost as a consequence of growth, as their realization of what is required changes with experience and also their perception of the resources they possess. As far as I can ascertain, the deliberate planned use of transformation is not yet a common occurrence.

I suppose that most of those who have presented problems to me have been people already well committed to the idea of working with groups. Even so, I would suspect that not to consider the question of why a group is a suitable instrument of work with people, both as a general idea and also in specific situations, is a symptom of enthusiasm obliterating the necessary act of assessment. All the effort which is concentrated in the literature on the preparation which is necessary before the start of a group is failing significantly if it does not promote answers to the primary problem of why using a group is considered to be the most effective means of procedure.

THE NATURE OF PROBLEMS IN GROUPS

I think a brief word may be necessary here about several important issues related to groupwork problems. In fact three main areas about the nature of such problems spring readily to mind:

1 Pattern recognition
2 Observer/actor bias
3 Problem or symptom?

1 Pattern recognition

One of the advantages of keeping some form of record of group sessions is that it becomes possible to see what looms as a problem in the context of the group's life. In fact it would be true to say that a major groupwork skill is that of being able to recognize patterns. One-off situations may be very rewarding or very traumatic and can thus influence the perception of the group and its leader out of all proportion to their long-term effect. It is not uncommon, therefore, that people are labelled as behaving in a particular way based wholly upon one exclusive but impressive performance. This then generates a self-fulfilling prophecy.

Usually problems are stated by groupworkers in a way that indicates they *are* describing something which in their experiences repeats. Indeed they are often relating various attempts to modify what they have seen as a bad pattern, most of which seem not to have succeeded in eliminating, reducing or changing that pattern. Another factor, which records rather more than fallible memory will show, is that the problem, whatever it may be, is embedded in, and occupies a particular relationship to, a sequence of events. This sequence may be one of events, physical or emotional, within or without the group. But as we shall see later, it is a crucial part of groupwork skill to be able to recognize what is happening in the group, and in order for this to take place with any degree of efficiency some level of information processing has to be developed. Some of this may be better understood by reference to feature analysis theory, though this is by no means a wholly agreeable approach.

In working with groups, if a worker pays attention to the way situations generate in his/her groups and notes the outcomes over a period of time, similar situations can be recognized in the early stages of their development. Apparently we recognize patterns which are similar by recognizing the presence of discrete parts of which the whole is composed and also by their relationship to each other and to the overall pattern. This is possible despite the fact that the parts may vary in any or all of their manifestations, for example, size, colour, intensity, and so on.

Finally we recognize a pattern in whatever form it occurs because it stands out clearly against the background in which it exists.

A very obvious example of pattern within a group which appears to have been universally noted is that of the developmental sequences. The level of recognition can range from the simplistic, for example, forming, norming, storming, and so on, which are usually linear, that is, each stage follows the one before it, to the essentially complex which allows for regression, stagnation and spiralling development.

Another point about pattern recognition is a familiar fact to all art students, that is, that it is possible to be trained to see things which other people do not see. Thus the world becomes a much more interesting place when having learned about theories of light the student realizes that self-colour on any surface is only a general effect and contains within itself so many different colours, tints and shades generally ignored by the unschooled. Finally it is the changing nature of recognized patterns over time which is the most reliable indicator of what is happening in a group. Logically change can only be measured against a baseline, which constitutes an excellent and solid reason for the early recognition of patterns and for the recording of them to form a basis for later comparison and review. In order to see any pattern which is larger than a dyadic interaction it becomes necessary to be able to stand back somewhat. This is more a psychological act than a physical one. It involves a deliberate choice to pay attention to the larger patterns of group life without ignoring the minutiae. That this is a difficult skill to acquire goes without saying, as there is little in our general maturational and educational patterns which adequately prepares us for this kind of surveillance. But two factors which are of immediate help are the recognition of *similarity* which lies at the base of *repetition*, which as we shall see tends to be ubiquitously present as the defining characteristic of the problems presented here.

2 Observer/actor bias

Given the evidence[2] which would indicate that the position from which a person observes or participates in an event has some considerable influence on that person's perception of the essential nature of the event, it becomes necessary to understand that all the material used here contains this sort of bias. Thus comments have been made by individuals about themselves and their own behaviour (as actors) or about others and their behaviour (as observers), and also as members of the group or as outsiders. It is one thing for a group leader to ask how to deal with a problem as he/she sees it of, say, the 'disruptive' member and quite legitimate, it is quite another to discover the opinion of the 'disruptive' member of the nature of his/her behaviour, and it may be even another again to discover the opinions of the other group members or of those outside the group.

Aside from the actor/observer effect it must be obvious that all the members of a group, while having some reasons in common for being there and having invested some energy and commitment to the group's avowed goals, also have other vested interests, some disclosed, others hidden, which affect the behaviour which they produce in the group setting. Thus it is as well to remember that a problem is a situation or sequence of events as perceived from one specific viewpoint, that is unless it has been presented, examined and discussed with others and a consensus arrived at concerning its nature. It is a frequent occurrence amongst group leaders that, having perceived a problem from their point of view, they feel a personal responsibility to resolve, diminish or change it, forgetting or not recognizing that the essence of group life is the sharing of all those factors which concern the group and to use all the appropriate resources which are available to it.

Of course there are some groups in which *group life* is small and in all groups there are times when it is less strong than at others. In which case the leader's sense of responsibility about his/her personal duty to deal with problems may well be highly necessary and appropriate. Then all those factors which make individual problem-solving and decision-making different from group decision-making and problem-solving will operate.

Example

The co-ordinator of a community mental handicap team believed that the performance of his team was being adversely affected by the lack of understanding the team members had of each other's roles. Given the comparative newness of the team this was a relatively reasonable assumption to make. Believing that as co-ordinator it was his personal responsibility to do something about this he made various attempts to improve the team's understanding of its role structure. These attempts did not meet with any conspicuous success and the team's performance remained poor and may even have deteriorated. When the team were asked to identify on paper their own roles and those of their colleagues in an exercise conducted by a non-team member, they were able to do so with a high degree of facility and accuracy. This led to a search for the 'real' cause of their poor performance which was eventually located in certain constraints imposed upon the team by the larger organizational system in which it was embedded.

3 Problem or symptom?

This section can be very brief because it is included mainly to remind readers that the way we describe a situation creates a very strong probability of the kind of way we will attempt to deal with it. In the example given above the co-ordinator saw the team's poor performance as a problem – one which he felt would be seen as his responsibility by his superiors. Thus he applied remedies and solutions to no avail. What he was actually looking at was a symptom of some quite considerable distress which manifested itself in a form of professional seclusion, each member staying quite safely within traditional professional boundaries and not daring to cross them, although as intelligent people they knew well enough that a multi-disciplinary team is usually set up to exploit shared resources. Thus many of the strategies discussed in this book start from the necessity of (a) clarifying the problem and then (b) checking with others that what has been assumed to be so is so for others as well.

A group leader may ask 'How do I cope with long silences?' Apart from any consideration of the context in which the long silences occur the leader's perception of their length and of their effect, that is, creating a problem, may be largely influenced by many other factors not least of which may be the leader's anxiety about his/her position *vis-à-vis* the group. Thus long silences may be a leadership problem, a group problem, or even an environmental influence problem, or possibly several of these factors all operating at once.

This should always be borne in mind when looking at possible strategies for coping with illustrated problems if those strategies are to remain as examples of technique based upon a sound knowledge of what is involved rather than as 'specific' or 'sure fire' remedies which can be applied like sticking plaster.

One final fact becomes very noticeable when the lists of problems presented here are scanned. Some problems are stated in such a way that it is clear that the presenter has worked hard at analysing what he/she found and may be quite clear that they have discovered the basic reasons for what they are presenting. The problem they are asking about is not the problem itself but what can be done about it. Of course their analysis may be incorrect, biased in some particular direction or ignorant of salient points, all of which must be considered. But if it is not any of these things then the strategy required is one for dealing with the 'known'.

Other problems are presented in a way which indicates a degree of puzzlement so that the strategy which is being asked for is of the nature of one which will help to discover what is actually occurring as at least a first stage and only then as a possible second stage to indicate how the problem may be dealt with.

This dichotomy is, as has been indicated, often clearly signalled in the form in which the problem statement is made.

THE PATTERN OF PRESENTATION AND THE EFFECTIVE METHODS OF USING THIS BOOK

It must be obvious from the sources of the problems discussed here that most will be concerned with some aspect of leadership if only because the majority of contributors are, or have been, or will be people working with groups. Thus only a small number of problems have been offered from the point of view of being a group member without designated leadership tasks and from people outside the group altogether, for example, managers, administrators, and others whose position is concerned with the functioning of the group as a part of a larger system for which they have some responsibility but who are not part of the group.

So the presentation here could have been reduced to one super category, that is, the problems of groupworkers. This monolithic approach, while fine in other respects, could have created problems of access to the material. Let me explain.

The problems as presented by groupworkers always have a specific focus. For instance a groupworker might say 'I have a problem with handling a particularly disruptive member in my group. How can I deal with this?' Of course disruptive members occur in a multitude of different forms and in widely different circumstances, but discussions with groupworkers quite frequently centre around the subject of 'the disruptive member'. Undoubtedly it is a groupworker's problem if only in so far as that having recognized that what he/she describes as 'disruptive behaviour' is inhibiting the group in achieving its aims. The fact that ultimately the groupworker's responsibility may lie in the direction of alerting the group to his/her perception of the consequences of this behaviour is a matter of choice of response and does not detract from the group-worker's perception of it as a 'problem'.

To make it easier for the reader to locate the material which might help him/her with a particular problem, what has been presented as the focus of each problem has become the basis here of the system of classification. Thus if we take the problem presented above, that of the disruptive member, it will be found in the section entitled 'Problems relating to the members of a group'. As group disruption is usually presented it is a form of member behaviour and thus the interested reader would need to look in Chapter 3.

In this category will be found a whole series of problems related to member behaviour and prominent amongst these will be that of behaviour which has as its apparent effect the disruption of the group process. Here will be found an analysis of this kind of 'problem' with the basic aim of discovering those elements of causation and patterns of use which are basic or common to all or at least most of such 'problems'.

Following this will be a presentation of those ideas which have been shown to have a value in enhancing the understanding of this kind of problem. For instance, in the case of disruptive behaviour it will be those concepts relating to the rationale of behaviour of this nature based upon the fundamental assumption that unless people have lost control of their behavioural responses, all behaviour is motivated to achieve some personally acceptable end product. Other ideas are equally explored which range all the way from deliberate malicious intent, which is relatively uncommon, through past experience, to security factors, to straightforward rational response to a perceived situation, however idiosyncratic.

The following section will present possible/probable strategies for dealing with these events bearing in mind the fundamentally different group situations in which an apparently similar pattern of behaviour can emerge. These strategies arrive directly out of the understanding of the problem vouchsafed by the concepts presented in the previous sections. For instance, where the problem may be one which involves the intense dislike some members of a group have for another member, one of the strategies available is based on the idea that such dislike is often based on readily visible difference. The strategy then is concerned to counter this effect by discovering and making plainly visible to the group, either through demonstration, the more effective method, or by discussion, those assets possessed by the disliked group member, skills, knowledge, and so on, which are of obvious proven value to the group.

In essence this may well bring about a recognition in the groupworker concerned that the preparation for a group does not cease when the group is brought together, but only diminishes when the group achieves the level of functioning and efficiency compatible with the goals it hopes to achieve. There is in a sense a considerable amount of nurturing to be done. A group is a 'function-in-time' in which the lives of the members meet for a while. If this meeting is repeated then the group may come to represent a situation of influence in the lives of its members.

THE RELATIONSHIP OF AN ANALYSIS OF COMMON PROBLEMS TO THE DEVELOPMENT OF GROUPWORK SKILL

The honing and refining of groupwork skill is a long-term process in which experience in a variety of group settings as well as time is very necessary. Any system may be said to be only as effective as the quality of response that it makes to the feedback that it receives. So in groupwork there is a constant need to discover how effective strategies which have been employed have actually been.

There is a great fog here which is thickened by the persistence of some people that attempting to analyse why a particular group was successful or not, or why some parts were good and others not, is coldblooded and inhuman. They maintain that the set relationships that are formed in the warmth and security of the group are not susceptible of analysis.

The warmth of groups is notoriously ephemeral, and unless some rational understanding of what has happened also occurs the chance that the experience will not transfer to the world outside the group without continuing support is great.

When a groupworker recognizes that something is happening within his/her group and seeks for ways to deal with it, the first action that is liable to occur is an analysis of what is actually happening. Now not only is this process a first and essential step in the process of deciding on a strategy, but it also provides a useful baseline against which, if it is duly recorded, any future change may be assessed.

Too often change in groupwork is based upon subjective impression either because the record of what occurs is inadequate or even non-existent. Thus the whole system of adjustment, progress and development based upon a clearly-plotted relationship between cause and effect is minimized if not negated. This can lead to the continuation of leadership patterns which are 'felt' to be effective, but for which little or no actual evidence of achievement can be adduced. As an apprenticeship system for the development of groupwork skills is a very unlikely possibility in this country, then some form of self-monitoring and self-regulation is of paramount importance as a counterbalance to the possibility of a growing self-satisfaction which may not be justified.

It is suggested therefore, that whenever a strategy is adopted the consequences of applying it in a group should be carefully recorded and monitored over a reasonable period of time. There is no certainty that the original diagnosis of the problem is correct and it must therefore be placed alongside the intervention and palpable consequences to discover how right it was. By this method of continuous accretion of successful leadership acts, a more sensitive and accurate approach to working with groups can be built up.

Many groups underfunction, they do not realize, let alone use, the resources which are available to them in anything like the degree to which such use may be possible. And yet we constantly affirm that one of the main reasons for creating and/or working with groups, is because they possess more and different resources than are usually available to any individual member. The principal cause of the underfunctioning may well have great similarity to the reason why groupwork skill is found to be so difficult to promote – namely that group-interested people appear to regard serious systematic investigation of a group as being in all probability destructive of what they must believe to be a fragile entity.

However, as far as I am aware, there is no evidence that this is so. Thus when groupworkers seek help for a problem or problems which are occurring in their groups, perhaps the last thing they should be offered is a remedy derived from the wisdom and experience of someone in a consultant role. What might be much more useful would be that the expression of a problem should be made the basis and reason for preparing a method of problem analysis and the ongoing development of a skill. Not an answer to a particular situation but a method for turning problems into enhanced effectiveness is what is required.

What this handbook attempts to do is show the probable stages of the application of just such a method, which, I must repeat, is founded upon the absolute need to keep reasonable records of what takes place. For it is some-times necessary to have quite long historical sequences available for scanning before connecting and causal linkages can be appreciated. Without this kind of sequential recording the development of the groupworker or team leader is indeed limited to the immediately visible effect of any action undertaken.

If the sources of help with common groupwork problems offered here are used effectively and a pattern of such use and feedback developed, then some, but not all, of the shortcomings of our 'methods' of developing groupwork skill beyond the basic competences may be overcome.

To reinforce the presentation of these strategies they are followed by some discussion which seeks to show the logical connection between a perceived problem, the analysis of causation and the consequence, the design of appro-priate strategy, its application and the monitoring of the result.

Finally there is a list of selected readings which are directly relevant to the problem area.

Let it be stated here very plainly that there is no intention of providing a bag of tricks or a set of games. On the contrary, the method by which the strategies presented here are arrived at is probably more important than the strategies themselves. The complexity of group behaviour renders it rather unlikely that any groupworker will find here the exact replication of his/her problem. What they will find in all probability, is something similar, but more importantly they will discover some of the information relating to problems of that kind and a reasonably explicit method for designing their own highly appropriate strategy.

This raises some problems with which I will deal in the next section.

STRATEGIES: THEIR NATURE AND USE

The word *strategy* used to mean 'generalship, art of war; art of planning and directing larger military movements and operations of a campaign or war' (OED) only, but in the context of use here it implies planning ways of coping with problems rather than responding purely on the basis of the urgent need to do something. Very experienced groupworkers who appear to respond to situations immediately have almost always acquired the ability to do so on the basis of a long period of having to think through their responses in the earlier days of their development.

So 'strategy' means a large element of logic and reasoning must precede a response which is then based on all, or as much as possible, of the available evidence. Such an element of reason does not imply slowness nor does it imply a total absence of emotion. Feeling is indeed an important evidential component. But there is another factor which must be made explicit here. There are occasions when the groupworker/team leader must respond to situations purely as an individual with special responsibilities, that is, alone. There are other occasions when to do so would be a total negation of one of the group's basic aims which is to be able to recognize, analyse and cope with its own problems as a unit using its known and available resources. Thus, although the leader may see the need for change, he/she must always assess the condition of the group as to whether he/she acts upon that perception directly or shares it with the group, thus encouraging others to do likewise.

Groups are often constructed on the basis of this dichotomy and usually designated as directive or non-directive. In my book all groups are 'directive'. The distinction lies in the perception of how, in given conditions, the group may most effectively achieve its stated aims. There is always an element of choice and I prefer it to be made pragmatically, rather than by a rigid adherence to a point of view, with the ultimate benefit of the group as the major point of reference.

Strategies can operate at different points of application; these I listed in *Group Processes in Social Work* (1979) as follows:

With individuals
With subgroups
With total group
With external factors (individuals, subgroups, groups, and so on)
In combination

Leadership or directive behaviour may be designed to operate in six major categories, namely:

1 Arrestive – to stop further action or situational involvement.
2 Reductive – to reduce the intensity of behaviour, of interaction.
3 Maintaining – to support without active encouragement.
4 Enhancing – to encourage, stimulate to produce more of the same.

5 Modifying – to change the behaviour or interaction in terms of:
        – its direction (backwards, forwards, sideways)
        – the focus
        – the emphasis.
6 Countervailing – starting a new process, subject, activity, and so on.

Any or all of these operations may be achieved verbally or non-verbally – a choice which can best be demonstrated graphically:

Example	Question	Particular event being considered
Observation	What is going on?	Member A has just made a first very tentative statement in the group
Assessment	Is this leading to the achievement of short-term aims? long-term aims?	Probably both. It would appear to be a good example of the freedom of all to contribute to the group in their own way
	Is it irrelevant? Is it leading away from group aims? Is it damaging?	No No No
Consideration of options	Do I need to do anything?	Yes – because this is a breakthrough as far as A's contribution to the group is concerned
	If Yes – directly? – indirectly?	No Probably as being less embarrassing
Decision*	How can I obtain action directed at member A from the group?	Stimulate the group to encourage member A* (see below)
Monitor	Are the responses to the action good, bad, or neutral?	The encouragement pleased member A and freed him to make further contributions

*At this point say the decision was to encourage member A, then the options open to the group-worker can be charted roughly as follows:
   to encourage member A.

	Directly (to A)	Indirectly (through the group)
V E R B A L	'That was good' 'Go on – that was very interesting'	'I think that what A has just said was exactly what was needed' 'We must consider with care the insight/information/contribution which A has just given us'
N O N V E R B A L	Smile Nod Gestures indicating to A to continue, physical action demonstrating approval of A's behaviour appropriate to its significance for the group	Gestures which elicit approval from the group for A

Often enough the approaches are combined, but separating them gives a greater control over the degree and direction of encouragement and they can be shaped to be appropriate to the group's assessed stage of development and to the individual's need.

Our society allows, even encourages and expects, statements and gestures of dis-approval to be at a greater level of use than statements and gestures of approval. To be approving actually requires positive expression and effort because withholding any sign either approving or disapproving is most often taken to imply an acceptance of the status quo or even of negative feelings.

There is a great need for the individual members of a group to become aware of the kind of phrases and gestures which they would normally use to express, say, encouragement, and to test them out on their current colleagues. *A currency with an unknown value is very difficult to use effectively.* What appears to have worked well in the past may not work anything like as well in a different situation because of the very different ways in which people respond and interpret what is offered.

Finally, a word about words themselves, which in our verbally-oriented society are the chief instruments of group interaction. The form of words which is used is crucial in conveying underlying intent. There are degrees of saying what might be assumed to be the same thing; thus:

1 'You are angry'   A statement with an element of challenge said as if it were an incontrovertible fact.

2 'You seem to be angry'   A statement which includes some reference to the speaker's perception.

3 'You behave as if you   A statement allowing of some doubt of the assump-
are angry'   tion underlying it.

4 'I think that you are   A statement referring to the speaker's thoughts
angry'   rather than to the person addressed.

5 'It seems to me that   A further move towards consideration of the person
you are angry'   who is speaking.

6 'I get the impression   This implies that the speaker is making known his/
from your behaviour   her impression and seeking for comparison with
that you are angry'   others.
. . . and so on.

The range here goes all the way from a fundamental assumption of inalienable accuracy of perception to a statement where the clarity resides in the description of what the speaker really knows, that is, how something affected him/her and in the process of looking for comparisons with the perceptions of any others involved.

The whole process of consensual communication is fundamental to all strategies. In these pages we will discuss methods of 'getting across' meaning to others using, for instance:

Role modelling .... Setting an example of desirable behaviour.

Explanation .... An attempt to relate something new or different to personal constructs which already exist.

Exhortation .... A form of verbal persuasion (not usually extremely effective).

Description .... Making what is going on visible to all so that the group works from a commonly held base of understanding.

Reflecting .... Feeding back into the group.

Exposing, Revealing,
Clarifying .... This can be asked for as a major contribution to enhancing understanding.

Expression of
understanding .... Making possible comparisons.

Confirmation................... Of perceptions.

Expression .... Of feelings and of point of view.

Discussion..................... Sharing perceptions, ideas, and so on.

I know that many people are concerned that the level of personal control which appears to be involved in these processes denies the feeling aspect of working with people and of course they are wholly entitled to their point of view. But I would maintain that few people are so sensitively equipped that they can afford to ignore what rationality has to offer in addition to their gifts.

To others this section must seem extremely basic, but then it is not to such experienced workers that this handbook is primarily directed, but to those who seek to gain increased competence in the fascinating world of groups for the benefit of those with whom they choose to work.

NOTES

1 See Gale Centre Catalogue, 1987/88, Loughton, Essex.
2 See, for instance, Jones and Nisbet (1971). In essence the actor tends to describe his behaviour as his response to the situation in which he finds himself; the observer tends to believe that the actor's behaviour stems from his personality.

REFERENCES

Bradford, L.P., Stock, D. and Horwitz, M. (1970) 'How to diagnose group problems', in R. T. Golembiewski and A. Blumberg (eds) *Sensitivity Training and the Laboratory Approach*, Itasca, Illinois, F. E. Peacock Publishers, 37. (First published in 1961.)
Douglas, T. (1979) *Group Processes in Social Work*, Chichester, John Wiley and Sons.
Jones, E. E. and Nisbet, R. E. (1971) *The Actor and the Observer: Divergent Perceptions of the Causes of Behaviour*, Morristown, NJ, General Learning Press, 1–16.

Part II

Common groupwork problems

Chapter 2

An explanation of the classification system

The main purposes of dividing the problems presented here into different categories are essentially two, namely:

1 To collect together those problems which had the same or similar sources.
2 To create a simple accessibility to the material for the reader.

The main problem with the material presented to me has always been that in a large number of items the specific basis of the problem has been difficult to establish. As most of the problems were presented by people who, in one guise or another, could be described as groupworkers, it would not have been wholly unreasonable to classify them all as manifestations of problems arising from leadership activity.

But it is equally obvious that although the problems were presented by 'leaders' and in fact concerned them greatly, especially in knowing what they ought to do about them, the problems were also more or less firmly rooted in one or more of five major areas, namely:

1 Group members
2 The group as a unit or system
3 The conditions under which the group operated
4 Leadership process (processes)
5 Supervision, training and development

However, some extra explanation of what can be expected to be included in these categories is essential plus some explanation of two rather awkward difficulties which arise. As I explained in the Introduction (pp. 9–11), problems have a distinctly different bias according to whether they are being stated by a person about him or herself, or about another, or about an incident, or a system. There is ample room for confusion. For example, many times groupworkers have felt that the comparative failure of their endeavours has been due to their lack of skill. In some cases this is undoubtedly true but in others it may well be the conditions imposed on the group of whose effects the workers are almost wholly unaware, which prevents their success.

The second difficulty lies in the way a problem is presented – not just in the viewpoint, for example, non-member, leader, and so on, but in the words used to describe what is happening. Taken individually and in isolation such word differences present little problem. The difficulty arises when comparisons and similarities are sought. As the basis of this endeavour is to establish just such similarities so that the remedies which have been used with success elsewhere can be applied in suitably modified form to the current problem – the word-form can present formidable difficulties.

I am afraid that without a laborious and cumbersome system of elaborate definition this difficulty can only be met by the assertion of an individual opinion and that is what I have chosen to do. The similarities which I offer here are based upon my own experience and knowledge and must be read in the light of this statement.

Briefly, as explained earlier, the classification system is as follows:

1 The five major problem areas are presented separately and their general properties discussed.
2 They are then broken down into two or more subcategories referred to as sections which are defined and commented on.
3 Each section is then illustrated by a selection of quoted problems.
4 An analysis is made of these problems to elicit fundamental strands.
5 A brief statement of useful ideas related to the problem is given.
6 Probable strategies for dealing with the problem under various circumstances are offered, followed by
7 a discussion of the problems and strategies within each major problem area, and finally
8 a list of reference material pertaining to the section.

This structure should allow any interested person to dip into the handbook at the point which apparently concerns them and to find there the information they seek.

THE CLASSIFICATION SYSTEM

Major problem areas	Category A	Category B	Category C	Category D
I MEMBERS	(i) Biographical (ii) Personality & attitude (iii) Abilities, resources & status (iv) Aims & goals	(i) Performance & behaviour (ii) Roles		
II GROUP	(i) Normative structure (ii) Subgroup structure (iii) Open/closed structure (iv) Role structure	(i) Measurement of change		
III CONDITIONS	(i) Organization & policy (ii) Setting (iii) Time	(i) Size (ii) Design		
IV LEADERSHIP	Knowledge	Skills	Performance	Aims & objectives

Each section (i), (ii), and so on, in each category will have the following subsections:

General area of problem
Examples of representative problems
Analysis of problems
Brief statement of relevant concepts
Presentation of possible strategies which could bring about amelioration, change or resolution in problem management
Discussion
Selected reading

Chapter 3

Problems relating to the members of a group

GENERAL AREA OF PROBLEM

A group most obviously is comprised of its members, so in essence all problems of working with groups must relate to the members of those groups. However, it is possible to isolate those problems of members which emanate directly or indirectly from the kind of structures they form or from the techniques of handling them.

Thus this section presents a constellation of problems which can be seen as occurring in two major categories:

A Those difficulties which arise directly or indirectly from the kind of people the members are, and
B those problems which occur as a result of what they do which affects the group process.

A complication of this simple dichotomy lies in whether the problems in either category are presented by members themselves, by group leaders, or by others outside the group but having some legitimate interest in it. Where the source is known in the problems covered here it will not only be acknowledged but the influence it may precipitate will be discussed.

Under member category A problems have been presented under the following subcategories:

A1 Biographical
A2 Personality and attitudes
A3 Abilities, resources and status
A4 Aims and goals

Under member category B problems have been presented under the following subcategories:

B1 Performance and behaviour
B2 Roles

These subcategories are, like all factors connected with group behaviour, interrelated and information found in one category could often with equal facility have been found in another.

PRESENTATION OF PROBLEMS CATEGORY A

A1 Biographical

Surprising as it may seem biographical and personality characteristics have not been studied very extensively in the small group literature . . . for those cases in which such variables have been studied there do not seem to be any pervasive or general propositions that emerge.

(McGrath and Altman 1966:56–7)

Definition and comment

In essence the biographical factors of members are those matters which are an essential part of their life history, for example, social class, culture, physical and mental attributes, social position, opinions, attitudes, experiences, age, sex, social background, education, intelligence, and so on. Such a wide constellation of factors may in itself be of little value. Indeed, from the problems which have emerged it is clear that only when biographical characteristics of members are very apparent or when distinct problems within the group are seen or felt to be directly related to such characteristics, is much made of them. This may well be the reason why, as McGrath and Altman indicated above, little general research has been done in this area. The fact that attitudes, opinions and behavioural patterns which are of great concern to groupworkers are formed during what might be termed the biography of members, does not stop them from being singled out and separated from the whole of which they are an integral part.

Examples of problems

Here are some examples of problems which have arisen from the 'biographical factors' of members:

'There are difficulties in trying to include members from very diverse groups, people of different backgrounds, abilities and ages.'

'We have problems with the "socially isolated" who are unaccustomed to joining in . . . in terms of motivating them to attend a group.'

'How do you get isolated and apathetic people together?'

'How does one deal with the difficulties posed by age difference; sex differences?'

'Girls face considerable problems in groups either in mixed or girls-only groups.'

'How to get people to the same starting point when they come from different backgrounds.'

Analysis of problems

All of these problems are concerned with 'difference' or 'diversity'. Most groups are brought into existence in order to deal with specific problems or difficulties which face their members. But in creating such groups it is not possible or even credible that the group can concern itself solely with just that basic problem or difficulty. Members bring into the group themselves what amounts to a person who contains the totality of their experience, genetic-endowment and learned behaviour. Thus selection, if it is even possible, on the basis of one aspect of the potential member's life can bring together a collection of individuals, which apart from the similarity of their problem, may be as diverse a group of people as one might expect in 'modern' society.

The fundamental problems for the groupworker are thus two:

(a) Given that selection is a possibility, how can it be used to ensure that within reason it enables the achievement of the group's aims rather than inhibits them?

(b) If selection either wholly or in part is not possible, what are the most effective ways of encompassing this fact and for maximizing the group's performance?

Useful ideas

There are many concepts related to the problems of difference or diversity. I will list and briefly discuss the more important ones here and show how they can lead to a satisfactory strategy for dealing with some aspects of this sub-category of problems:

Interpersonal attraction	Those factors which cause people to like one another and which can cross the boundaries of difference.
The known effects of diversity	Those factors which records show are most likely to emerge from different social groupings.
Cohesion	Those factors which allow a group to function effectively in the performance of its task by creating an appropriate area of consensus, so that in those areas (and maybe in those areas alone) the group acts as a united system.
The theories of selection	A highly controversial area ethically and practically, given the low and often inaccurate information levels we possess about potential members.

Time	Perhaps the most essential ingredient to understand – developing an appropriate working compatibility requires adequate time to effect as well as the necessary skill.
Law of cost/reward	The perception of satisfaction obtained from group membership is an important factor in commitment.
Trust	Not an easy concept to define and in groups the level of trust needs to be appropriate and relevant to the stage of development the group has reached and ultimately to the goals which it has accepted. Trust is commonly defined in a rule of thumb manner as the ability to predict with reasonable accuracy the response of other members to behaviour produced in the group.
Group development	If a collection of individuals develops into a functioning system then it is to be expected that difference and diversity will elicit changed responses in the group as stages of development are reached, passed or not reached.
Structure	As structure is dealt with more fully elsewhere in this handbook it must suffice to say here that known structure can provide acceptable and accepted functional slots for group members in which their diversity and difference is of little if any negative significance for the group.
Individual values and status	The value or worth that a member holds for a group can often be set against any negative impact from perceived difference.

Strategies for problems relating to biographical factors of group members

Strategies for this area of membership problems may be designed under the following headings:

(a) Selection–non-selection
(b) Structure
(c) Worth/value/status/relationships
(d) Positive energy – relating to diversity and conflict, the aims, existence and purpose of the group

It must be remembered that there are two crucial factors involved in difference or diversity of members:

That diversity is, or can be, one of the major resources of the group – the problem lies in discovering what those resources are in terms of knowledge, experience, understanding, skill, and so on, then in making them known to the group, and finally in devising methods for their use. Thus diversity productively utilized is a huge positive asset.

That diversity/difference becomes destructive or inhibiting in a group when it becomes more important to the members than the actual purpose for which the group was established.

It must also be remembered that all strategies can probably be assumed to be based in either of two approaches:

Those aimed at changing the situation, for example, the rules, the numbers, the location, methods of approach, and so on.

Those aimed at changing members' perception of a situation which, for whatever reason, is deemed to be in itself unchangeable, for example, changing the group's estimate of the value of a member whose 'normal' group behaviour has caused him/her to be ignored, by disclosing that he/she has assets of value to the group.

One final point is that whereas the recognition of a problem and the need for a strategy to cope with it may well be the responsibility of the group leader, the choice of the method of implementation will depend upon the stage of the group's development and on whether it is leader-directed or self-directed. The consequence of presenting a strategy which ignores these factors is usually negative.

Example

A group which had existed for a number of years developed a problem of an extremely dominating couple of members. The groupworker encouraged the group to confront this problem but the group consistently refused to do so. Individual members would discuss the need for action outside the group and complain to the groupworker, but no ingroup action was taken. When looking back over the history of the group it was easy to see why. No major decision taken by the group in its life had been taken except by the group-workers directly or indirectly. Many decisions had been made by the group but from their point of view they were always of minor importance, but they had disguised the stage of development of the group from the group-worker.

The first thing to look at is the possibility of preventing biographical diversity turning into a problem in the first instance, which fundamentally means looking at the strategy of selection and the kind of information which is available on which a groupworker can make a rational choice.

(a) Selection/non-selection

Is a wide diversity of members an essential design element in the proposed group?

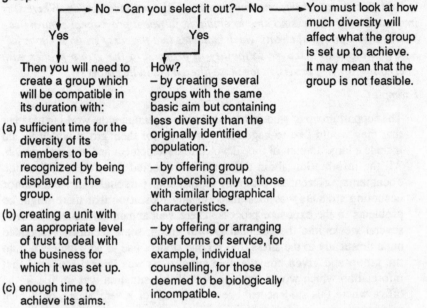

No – Can you select it out?— No ⟶ You must look at how much diversity will affect what the group is set up to achieve. It may mean that the group is not feasible.

Yes

Yes

Then you will need to create a group which will be compatible in its duration with:

(a) sufficient time for the diversity of its members to be recognized by being displayed in the group.

(b) creating a unit with an appropriate level of trust to deal with the business for which it was set up.

(c) enough time to achieve its aims.

How?
– by creating several groups with the same basic aim but containing less diversity than the originally identified population.

– by offering group membership only to those with similar biographical characteristics.

– by offering or arranging other forms of service, for example, individual counselling, for those deemed to be biologically incompatible.

The essential point is that if diversity of any of the biological factors is either necessary, for example, to obtain different experiences or viewpoints about a common issue, or unavoidable, for example, in working with a family as a group system, then adequate time for the group to recognize the diversity that exists and to devise methods of exploiting it for the benefit of the group as a whole, or to recognize what limitations such diversity will probably place upon the group's ability to achieve its goals and to modify those goals accordingly, is of fundamental importance.

Many problems related to biographical diversity arise in groups because insufficient attention was given to the possible effects such diversity might have. Then workers are faced with the necessity of having to deal with a problem, say, of age, gender or cultural difference or of social background, which need not have arisen. The main point to make is that of the learning which should come from such problems in terms of the increased skill in group creation and design or in recognizing the constraining effects of such factors.

Information quality   A decision is only ever as good as the information upon which it is based, and the quality of the information which is often available to groupworkers about prospective group members ranges from precise and exhaustive detail about the problem aspect to virtually nothing much at all about the person as a human being. This is frequently caricatured when people are referred to not by name but by the nature of some problem they possess, for example, he's diabetic, or a mugger, or a marital problem.

Push for increased information relevant to the proposed group. Where it is inaccessible, or there is no time to obtain it, maybe a provisional contract can be made with potential clients which indicates that the early group sessions will be exploratory to discover suitability to proceed to the group proper with alternative forms of provision for those filtered out in this process.

Example

The support group of students decided after several months working together that they would like to negotiate a contract for their group which would include a large amount of time devoted to development and personal growth. All the information about the students collected from their application documents, references, progress reports and personal experience since becoming students was examined for any indication that there might be problems in the exposure process. There was apparently none. However, several weeks into the personal growth group, some members responded quite drastically to the stress. Indeed one student had to be withdrawn from the group and given considerable support. It was later discovered that information which would have prevented this situation was on file in the office where this student had been employed for several years, but which was never communicated to the course.

(b) Structure

This can be used as a framework into which people can slot and which can give them a known and acceptable role and a purpose. It is often the only viable strategy to enable people to work together who have little ability to make and maintain personal relationships with one another or who have learned to be extremely frightened and wary of such relationships.

A very simple method of creating a task structure goes like this:

The group meets and a discussion takes place about what kind of jobs are necessary to get the group off the ground. These tasks may be extremely simple like the arrangement of furniture, preparation of refreshments, clearing-up, writing notices, offering lifts or help for those who may have difficulty arriving at the group, to much more complex and difficult tasks like keeping notes of the proceedings, taking responsibility for introducing new members or the subject for an activity session. These tasks are then taken on by members of the group.

Each of these tasks needs to be acknowledged and regarded by the group as a whole. The essential factor which emerges is that group members come to regard each other as having something to contribute which, because of its practical nature, offers little challenge to the fear of personal relationships but provides a basis from which that fear can be allayed.

A simple task structure can eventually be developed into a role structure in which members can begin to use their personal resources for the benefit of the group. Role structures are often difficult for group members to grasp except in the sense of 'he always responds like that'. But they are much easier to grasp as a development from a task structure.

Role structure will be considered in more detail in the next section so it is only necessary to say here that there are many categories of potential group members for whom some basic structure is necessary, something which they know about and which can provide some security and safety in what otherwise might appear to have all the elements of a very frightening situation. As far as possible the structures used should have a high level of relevance to members' pre-group experience.

(c) Worth/value

Worth is not always, or even often, a self-evident commodity. Thus, again, an extremely necessary and simple strategy is to signal its presence. In our society little attention is paid to commending the good facets of behaviour but much is given to the exposure of the bad by criticism and comment. Encouragement is therefore a rewarding situation but it often needs to be accompanied by a simple explanation of why the behaviour is being recommended, for example, 'I think that X's action was very timely because it brought us back to what we really should be doing and has probably saved us from wasting considerable time'.

Value has to be signalled When a group really begins to work efficiently together, it is largely because all its members have accepted that certain values, the worth of certain members, is essential for the group to function whatever values they continue to hold.

Often people, especially those with low self-esteem, fail to appreciate that they have much of value. Indeed life may have taught them exactly the opposite. It must therefore be a strategic move on the part of the group leader to attempt to discover what are commonly called 'strengths' of the group members and to make it his/her business, not to advertise these but to create opportunities for their display and use. 'To create' may be too obvious a method, but some such expedient must be used to prevent the peripherization of some members if opportunities to display and use their resources do not arise naturally.

Example

A team composed of professionals from several different disciplines were having considerable difficulty in designing a combined recording system which, while apposite for them as a functioning unit, was also acceptable to the different professional organizations which employed them. One of the newer team members who was yet little regarded by the others, revealed in an exercise in making personal resources visible, that one of his major pastimes was as the creator of computer programs, an occupation in which he proved to have considerable skill. The team leader asked whether he would be able to devise a program to meet their recording needs. He assured them it would be possible and thereupon that almost peripheral member became extremely important to the team because of his heretofore unsuspected expertise.

The primary bases of the strategy here are two:

1 If incidents which expose members' worth are occurring as a natural part of the group progress it is still necessary to highlight and explain them, or
2 If such incidents are few, to create deliberately small situations in which known but unexposed resources may be revealed. *A common enough axiom is that a group cannot use resources it does not know that it possesses.*

(d) Positive energy

It is often assumed that conflict in a group is destructive. This statement has to be qualified.

Conflict may be dangerous in a group at certain times, that is, in the early stages of development, during periods of transition from one stage to another, when the group is running down either because it has finished what it set out to achieve or because it has failed, when major changes of membership or leadership are taking place, when several of these factors are present either together or in a very close time sequence. Otherwise conflict is natural and a source of energy potential which can and should be used.

However, since conflict is dealt with at greater length elsewhere in this book (see pp. 64–8), I propose to concentrate here on other energy factors.

Gruen (1979) describes a leader strategy for developing positive energy use, which involves 'borrowing' the energy of the leader. This strategy is one in which the leader invests his/her energy, surplus that is to that which is required to maintain a steady state, for the use of the group members.

Example

A group of hostel residents had, over a period of months, suffered considerable set-backs which had, individually and collectively, reduced their self-esteem and their social competence to a very low point. One of the contributory factors had been the loss of an extremely charismatic house leader and a long gap before his replacement arrived. The new leader skilfully used his own energies to create a situation in which the residents began to relate to each other, replacing the previous system of each resident having a relationship to the leader with one in which each was demonstrably dependent on the others and they on him. This was achieved by each resident taking on some part of the overall responsibilities and duties of the establishment and all residents being encouraged into group meetings and into the decision-making process.

Gruen describes the process as being 'similar to augmenting the strength of a weak car battery by coupling it on to a stronger while starting the engine'.

A2 Personality and attitudes

Definition and comment

A large part of what group members bring with them into a new group consists of what may be defined very widely as their personalities and their attitudes. It is difficult to define or to make distinction here between the behaviour and the roles of group members which are often seen as the visible manifestations of personality and attitudes and the personalities and attitudes themselves. Where problems arise which appear to be inexplicable in terms of the current situation, that is, within the group, it frequently occurs that such problems are attributed to the personalities and/or the attitudes of those who are apparently creating the problems. Thus the examples quoted here are a very mixed bunch indeed (see introduction – fourth section).

Examples of problems

'I know adolescents need to receive adult attention, but how can I increase the interaction of youngster to youngster?'

'How do I get depressed, isolate and apathetic people to work together?'

'How do I deal constructively with dominant group members?'

'Some members become dependent on the group.'

'Problems occur because members have personality difficulties.'

'Some members have immensely different energy levels.'

'Members seem to have reasons for being in the group which are not related to the group task.'

'Some members are suspicious and lacking in trust.'

'There is an attitude which can be summed up as "we've tried it all before and it didn't work".'

'Some members have a very low motivation.'

Some groupleaders are much more explicit:

In this group I work alone and the group members make it quite clear that they will not accept other professionals sitting in or tape recording. They see the group as one in which they help themselves and in which well-established members help new ones – left to their own devices they rarely talk about themselves in any depth and are inconsiderate, even hostile, to new members. They are a self-selected group who come because they still need the group but some of them claim that they come mainly to help others. I need to know whether to confront them on their unacknowledged need for staff help or to allow them to continue to feel they run their own self-help group.

Analysis of problems

These problems are also concerned with difference and diversity but there are some subtly unique factors involved. Personality and attitude are almost inevitably seen as negative. Thus no groupworker ever comments on having a problem with a personality which is a positive asset to the group, nor on member attitudes which powerfully influence the group's direction unless they become, or appear to become, a challenge. Thus dominant personalities are a remarkably common problem as are apathetic members who will make absolutely no commitment to the group and its work – yet continue to attend.

Right at the outset it must be said that not a few people find being a member of a group, especially if it was not their specific choice to attend in the first place, a fairly threatening experience.

Thus we have problems relating to at least four major categories:

1 What may be called the defining category of member, for example, adolescent, depressed, isolate, and so on.
2 Personality factors, for example, dominance, energy levels.
3 The personal aims of members as they relate to individual attitudes.
4 Attitudes, for example, suspicion, lack of trust, low motivation of the 'seen it all before' kind.

Useful ideas

All information concerned with the states of human beings	Obviously it is not possible for any one person to have great knowledge of many states but at least each groupworker should know where to obtain the kind of information currently needed either in literature or from people with the requisite knowledge.
Behaviour patterns	There is a great deal of literature about personality and the behavioural patterns which ensue, which should be consulted.

Those ideas relating to authoritarian attitudes and concepts of social power.

The formation, development and changing of attitudes	Attitudes are not opinions and are much, much less susceptible to rational argument – it is necessary to understand the nature of the emotional power which sustains attitudes before any influence or change can be instigated.
Protective behaviour	This may well have been learned and originally successful in application, but may be a relic from the past.
Motivation	Usually measured as the degree of commitment – basically people will commit energy to those situations which, in their view, are liable to create at least some reward which appears greater than the energy committed to obtain it. This is often referred to as 'the balance of satisfactions'. The problem is that it is usually very difficult to know what constitutes a 'satisfaction' for any individual. Rewards in this sense are extremely individual and often inaccessible to others.
Trust	As a rule of thumb, basic trust between group members may be said to exist when they have sufficient experience of one another's behavioural responses to be able to predict with reasonable accuracy what those responses will be in the more commonly met-with situations, both in quality, kind and intensity.
Hidden and personal agendas	There is a collection of ideas surrounding the fact that all group members have at least several reasons for being there – some of which they are prepared to be open about, some are hidden but known to the individual, and some may be unknown even to the individual (in this case they are hardly 'reasons' in the usual sense, but may be very compelling needs). All these factors govern behaviour, commitment, and so on, and their outcomes are quite frequently attributed to other, more visible influences.
Attitudes	Attitudes are in essence frames of reference and influence and the way we judge and react to people, events and objects. They are thus very important. They are usually stable, they are learned, and because of their central role in the

Cognitive dissonance

use we make of them to impose sense upon our world, they are very difficult to change.

Briefly cognitive dissonance occurs when an incident disrupts the state of balance of conson-ance in which all the attitudes of an individual are usually maintained. The uncomfortable ten-sion which the dissonance generates provides the necessary energy and motivation to restore the balance which involves changing an attitude or attitude component to be more in line with the rest of the system.

Strategies

Categories

A large number of groups are formed on the basis that the members display the characteristics which are common to a particular category of being, personality, problem, behaviour, and so on. Thus a group could consist of people who had recently suffered bereavement, or been placed on probation, and so on. Yet categorical selection, while allowing of concentration on a selected area of exis-tence, entails problems, not least in the intensification of that area of exper-ience.

Strategies must take this factor into careful consideration.

Selection

Where selection is possible and it must be remembered that the reason for com-bining people into a group to cope with a particular area of their lives by direct implication means that large areas of their existence are untouched by the problem, wherever possible, information about potential group members should be acquired and members chosen on the basis of the resources which will most apparently be available to work with in the prime area of focus.

Example

A group of adults who had problems stemming from experience of sexual abuse as children were selected into a group on the basis of three categories: those who were grossly distressed by their early experiences; those who had apparently coped with the problem; and one or two who had received help earlier and were coping in a different kind of way. This selective mix was chosen so that the resources available to the group of ways of dealing with their kind of difficulties covered a wide and positive set of experiences.

Group design

The group must be built around the specific categorical issues which entails that the basic factors which promote and sustain the behavioural category must be as thoroughly understood as is possible and carefully matched by aspects of the group process both in the short and the long term.

Example

'How do I get depressed, apathetic and isolate people to work together?'

All three terms used in this quotation are descriptions of overt behaviour patterns which may relate to all aspects of an individual's life or only to specific areas of it. The first part of any strategy regarding such people must be *to get more information* about what promotes and sustains that behaviour. The second must be to carefully consider what group dynamic will be, not only acceptable but will promote and nurture changes. Fundamentally all three characteristics mentioned here operate against effective inclusion in a group. Therefore a group designed to deal with these problems has to initiate the process of *becoming a group* in a much longer and slower time-scale than would be usual, working with people in pairs and triads through common interest, liking or whatever attracting factors might be available. Obviously much time has to be spent in locating these factors and also those which could be used to promote the target behaviours.

It must be mentioned here that group design has to take cognizance of those group dynamics which may develop which are antipathetical as well as those which are positively promotive of changed behaviour. Fundamentally, the behaviours in question here have developed because the person has found, for whatever reason, that they arose or were produced in the first place, to be a more acceptable accommodation to particular aspects of his/her life than any other of which he/she is aware of being capable of performing. Thus the design of any group attempting to cope with these problems must be even more concerned than ever to provide tangible rewards (in the terms of what the individuals concerned would regard as rewards) for the expenditure of effort. Getting such individuals to 'work together' would ultimately depend for success upon what value was placed upon the proposed 'work' by the potential group members in view of their own estimate of the energy they had available.

To repeat. The basic strategy is one which is concerned with collecting sufficient information of good quality and in the process of matching the group design with that information.

Example

A group which was established for single mothers who had received attention or treatment for depression was established with extreme care and a great amount of forethought. A nursery was provided for the children, initial interviews were on an individual basis and agreement to attend was elicited.

Timing, programme and all the factors of design that were known about were explored. But out of eight or nine who had agreed to attend only three actually turned up for the first group and this was later reduced to two. Through follow-up, the groupworkers discovered a whole series of factors which influenced willingness to attend and which they had never anticipated:

1 Several had agreed to attend because the group had been recommended by their doctor and they had felt compelled to agree, but their lack of real interest kept them away when the pressure was off.
2 Many couldn't face the exposure they thought would be an essential part of being in a group and although agreeing to attend when face to face with the convenors had had no real intention of submitting to what they deemed would be an uncomfortable situation.
3 As depressives their lack of energy meant that inertia took over.

This is a clear indication of the need to be aware of the costs to a potential group member IN THEIR TERMS and the need to offer some potential reward again IN THEIR TERMS which would make their costs a viable expenditure of a scarce resource.

Dominance, high energy levels

The main problem about the dominant, high energy group member is that he/she introduces a level of incompatibility into the group. When 'dominance, vigour, adventuresomeness, purposefulness, orderliness, self-determination and freedom from anxiety' are high in a group then it really shows a high level of co-ordination of task performance and doing rather than talking (Hartford, 1971:119).

So there are two particular areas of possible problem:

1 Where high dominance levels create a group which is action-oriented when its purpose is really to be basically discussive.
2 Where dominant members and non-dominant members are in such proportion that incompatibility results.

Acknowledgement

A strategy which acknowledges the drive and energy of the dominant group members is the first step. The second is to clarify where that dominance is leading. Most groupworkers do not grumble about dominant members if their energy appears to be moving in the direction the group wants to go. If domination is an habitual pattern of behaviour irrespective of the end to which it is directed, other than self-security, and there appears to be no way of directing the energy to serve the group purpose, then removal from the group for the benefit of the others, preferably to some other form of care, may be the only viable strategy.

Example

In a group of ex-patients of a psychiatric hospital one male member who had a record of being a powerful dominating person consistently pushed the group to move forward at a speed which was highly incompatible with the needs of most of the members. His energy was acknowledged by the group and its leader and occasionally it was put to good use on behalf of the group. But over several months neither the group nor its leader could convince this member of the disastrous results of his insistent behaviour until other members began to absent themselves as protest and protection. The only remaining strategy for the group leader was removal of the offending member to the care of a colleague on a one-to-one basis.

It is well to remember that domination is in effect the controlling of the behaviour of others; most dominators tend to feel that their basic internal organization is more perfectly functional and structured than the internal organization of others. It is always necessary to measure all strategies against this fact as also as to whether the dominance is exercised through the medium of the physical, through apparent expertise or through charisma. But in all cases the final aim of any strategy must be to attempt to use the dominator's drive as a positive benefit and only when this fails to take steps to protect the group.

Personal aims

All members have personal aims in joining a group. The fact that these may not be identical or even similar to those which are generally accepted as being the aims of the group, often means that they are never publicly exposed. The problem in this case is that they continue to influence the group's and the members' achievements in ways which are often inexplicable to others.

Reality strategy

This implies ensuring that the group members are assured that all the reasons, purposes and aims which brought them into the group, and which may influence their behaviour, are admissible. The technique involved is to be able to highlight the difference between *knowing* that possible influences exist and actually taking action on that knowledge.

Example

In a group of civil servants members were intended to have chosen to attend on their own initiative because of the required increase in understanding of some complex issues which could arise in their work. During the process of working it became clear that the motivation of some members was much weaker and different to others. When the group leader presented the idea that it might well be that some members had been 'drafted' into the group by their superiors and that this was a reality that could be worked with, several members admitted that such was the basis of their attendance at the group. This caused a marked relaxation in the group atmosphere. Being 'drafted' was legitimate and allowed the drafted members to take some active part in the group proceedings.

Some personal aims are almost wholly inimical to the progress of a group and the members possessing such aims may well have to be removed from the group on the basis that the group usually exists for the benefit of the greatest number.

Lack of trust/suspicion

Given that trust appears to be founded on the basis of knowing what to expect from others in a given situation, that is, some sense of security through being prepared, then strategies concerned with increasing trust must endeavour to enhance that kind of knowing. Certain kinds of behaviour of leaders and of members are known to enhance suspicion and should be noted so that in the early stages of providing the basic knowledge of what to expect they can, as far as possible, be reduced to a minimum. These behaviours are as follows:

1 Critical evaluations and assessments of what is going on.
2 Obvious control – the exercise of arbitrary power.
3 Indication that the group's existence in ALL its aspects has been planned and will be strategically followed whatever happens.
4 Obviously neutral behaviour on the part of those who are believed to know what is going on and are seen to possess the power to affect change.
5 Clear indications of superiority with the inference or implication of inferiority for others.
6 Purveying the feeling of being very certain of oneself and of one's actions.

It is not intended that these six behaviours should be avoided like the plague. On the contrary, all have their uses and some, like neutrality, have been built into a complete approach. What must be understood is that these behaviours, especially in the early days of a group, *generate defensive suspicions and untrusting responses*. Does feedback about your personal line as leader indicate the necessity for caution in any of these areas? It is very easy to use several of these behaviours to mask one's own anxiety and uncertainty.

Conversely, there are those behaviours which effectively generate a supportive response. Briefly these are:

1 Descriptions of things, people, actions which are as objective as may be and serve to create a visualization of some clarity for those who may well become confused by the complexity of the group situation.
2 An orientation of the group towards those problems which the group regard as of prime importance and can be encouraged to address. This is not to say

that this procedure should take absolute priority over whatever task the group may have as its agreed objective should it be different, but groups notoriously will not devote themselves to work until certain basic criteria of security and understanding have been established. As these may have to be established by experience and observation rather than by explanation, this can take some time depending upon the degree of group-sophistication of the members.

3 The encouragement and acceptance of being spontaneous and of demonstrating that spontaneous responses have a high correlation with honesty and sincerity and thus with the development of openness and consequently of trust.

4 Behaviour directed to establishing some understanding of what the world looks and feels like from the position of others – this is a difficult procedure, but is paramount in developing in individuals a sense that their personal and idiosyncratic world is accepted by others and that some real effort is being made to understand it.

5 This behaviour is often described as the exercise of 'equality' and indeed it is difficult to describe any other way. But as obvious inequalities exist it has to be behaviour which values people for their humanity while accepting that difference and diversity are common, or can be common, positive factors.

6 While accepting that there is a considerable degree of predictability about what will happen in a group, there has to be a strong sense that it is possible and exciting to adapt to the unexpected. Immutability allows no one to have any sense of being able to extemporize, to experiment, to fail.

Direct expression of these behaviours can take some of the following forms:

Modelling   By being and behaving in some of the ways indicated above, an unequivocal model of how it can be done may be established.

Inhibit moralizing – about members' behaviour – words like 'ought' and 'should' when spattered freely through verbal interchanges are often a clear indication of moralizing taking place.

Resist the urge to shut people up – it may have to occur sometimes – but listening can generate a model not only of tolerance but that others have a right to be heard even if their method of presentation leaves a lot to be desired.

Be open to feedback – what you are being offered is some understanding of how you appear to others, your acceptance, and above all use of what you receive, will clearly indicate whether you intend to operate by the same rules of behaviour as the group or abide by a special set of rules for group leaders only.

Gently push wider the areas of trust – by creating opportunities for members to be dependent upon each other and thus finding from experience how few are the occasions of 'let-down'. Create opportunities for members to work effectively together, maybe in a subgroup – discuss and share openly common events, common experiences – reward trusting behaviour and acknowledge those differences which exist.

Expose members' game-playing activities – not because they are games but because they are patently manipulative and lack sincerity.

Security tends to reside in familiarity which in turn arises from repetition – widening of trust requires that movement from the known and safe to the new and unknown shall be gradual and not in such large steps that the lack of security promotes regression to the previous secure state.

A3 Abilities, resources and status

Definition and comment

The abilities of members are resources but there are also resources of know-ledge, skill and understanding plus all those resource-like areas to which members have access. So resource in this context means very broadly anything to which members have access which could be of value to the group or team in pursuit of its legitimate agreed goals. Status comes into this equation simply because those members who are seen as possessing high status, that is, greatest worth to the group, are usually those whose resources and ability to use them on behalf of the group, including the resources of others, are greater either in quantity or importance than those of their peers. That this perception of worth may be wrong and based upon fallacies has been frequently demonstrated by research, but this in no way invalidates the ability of those *regarded* as having prestige to behave in less conforming ways and so directly and indirectly to bring about change in the way a group operates. One of the major problems in this field is to discover abilities and resources and after that to make them available for the group's benefit.

Examples of problems

'Some members appear to have closed minds.'

'Some members appear to have an inability to be objective.'

'Some members have an inability to listen.'

'Drop-outs tend to be those with fewer personal and social resources and thus in greater need – it appears to be a social class difference.'

'The members of this group have a great deal of relevant experience and knowledge but they think it is of little worth and won't offer it to the group.'

'How do you gain access to all the resources which are known to the members of this group?'

'Why do the "high-status" members of this team give the impression that we have little to contribute?'

'It seems that teams are formed on the basis of their professional skills and training, but often the more essential contributions to team functioning could come from their individual and personal abilities, contacts and interests.'

Analysis of problems

When it is said that the resources which a group possesses constitute one of the major reasons for working with groups, the corollary that these resources are difficult to ascertain let alone use is seen to be very important. In any group the resource pool that it constitutes is rarely known except when, over a long period of time, the group has faced a number of difficulties and resources within the group have been produced to meet them. Thus, to ask what resources and abilities exist within a group usually elicits little useful information – resources are almost always seen as directly related to the purpose for which they are to be used. Many of the problems like those stated here seem to stem from a general acceptance that it is possible to list resources, abilities, and so on, almost as an abstract exercise. But like the perception of status within a group, resources and abilities tend to be known about because at some time they have been demonstrated or discovered in response to a need to deal with a particular situation. Thus these qualities of members can only be elicited in terms of experience.

Example

A multi-disciplinary team were having a great deal of difficulty in creating a record system which would meet their common need for a central data bank while not ignoring the needs of the separate professional organizations to which they belonged. The answer was to set up a computer system with coded differential access. When the problem was clarified in this way one member declared that he possessed the necessary software design skills as part of his hobby to create such a system. Until the problem was made explicit the resource in the group to deal with it remained undeclared.

Thus there seems to be four major problem areas:

1 Abilities or rather the lack of ability in certain crucial areas.
2 Resources – social, professional, human.
3 Status – which seems to be indicated as defining the reality of what is to be expected in terms of resources and abilities.

4 Worth – some people do not seem to value their own experience greatly and probably value high status people too much.

Useful ideas

Self-esteem   Life has taught many people to accept what might be called incorrect or rather inappropriate evaluations of themselves – because experience of living is common does not mean that it is identical. Our society seldom rewards people sufficiently or in reasonable manner for what we do well, but it does criticize, often quite destructively and with a great sense of righteousness, those behaviours, attitudes, and so on, which are deemed 'wrong'. This is a crucial factor because many people possess skills, aptitudes, abilities, knowledge, experience which could be of immense value to others seeking ways to survive, yet it is not available to them because the people who possess such resources do not estimate them at all highly and seldom realize the value they may have for others.

Ability   As we shall see, many strategies are based in simply discovering what useful contribution members can make to group life – most of the abilities noted here by their lack are social skills and competences which the fortunate have acquired either because others offered the opportunity to do so or because the individual made a conscious decision to learn them. It is not possible to learn to listen, for instance, if few people ever bother to talk to you. Nor is it easy to be objective when no one has ever demonstrated its advantages. Of course, some abilities seem to be a natural development for some people and some are genetically handicapped.

Resources   These are usually only noted as and when they are used except for those whose skill, knowledge and ability are absolutely essential to their existence and who have usually had a long period of training. But even here the obvious swamps and obscures most of the other resources, for example, patience, kindness, ability to make warm relationships, and so on. The answers given to the question 'What have you got to offer?' are usually firmly linked to three factors, that is, self-esteem, experience and training.

Status   Usually implies being held in high regard – research into this phenomenon indicates that high status group members are allowed greater freedom to be different, tend to be the centres of communication patterns and thus more frequently exercise more influence on decisions, direction and progress. But like

power, status is awarded to some group members on the perceptions of others that it is appropriate – perceptions can change.

Class

Class is used here in the sense of defining the opportunities and
access that people have to learning appropriate social competences. As the term 'streetwise' makes us aware, what is
highly appropriate in one area of our society may be much less
so in another. It is almost always useless to award a higher
status to some forms of social competence than others. It may
be very useful to make explicit the basic rules under which
different social competences function.

Commitment,
expectation
and security

Group members, like everyone else, usually act as individuals,
that is, in what they deem to be in their own best interests. In
order to have access to the resources each individual brings to
each group situation they enter, there has to be a perception
that to offer something of themselves other than mere physical
presence in the group, and that their expectations of receiving
something of value in return, and that this process of giving
and getting is one in which the risks, although tangible, are
worth taking.

Holding

For an individual voluntarily to adjust his commitment in some
measure, no matter how small, in favour of the group, requires
that the individual should have assured him/herself by observing the behaviour of his/her co-members in the group situation,
not only that it is safe to do so, but that it is acceptable, desirable and ultimately rewarding both to the individual and the
group. The concept of 'holding' relates to the efforts made to
keep the group in functioning existence for however long it
takes for this assurance to develop.

Strategies

Abilities

Like resources, abilities are related to experience, though unlike resources they
seem to be more easily defined by group members. This is probably because
abilities are a more open part of our society and related to achievement. The
usual form of discussion seems to be concerned with lack of ability rather than
abundance.

The first strategy must be directed to recognition, because in many instances
group members may not be aware of what abilities exist. Take some of the
problems listed at the head of this section, for example, inability to be objective,
or to listen.

1 Both being objective and having the ability to listen are learned behaviours. The first move must be to discover whether members demonstrating either of these behaviours are aware, that is, that they are consciously emitting such behaviour because they choose to, or not. If they are not conscious of emitting such behaviours then the strategy must be for them to get feedback from the group that this is what they are seen as doing. This must be very carefully judged with a high degree of consideration for the person concerned. It must not be highly critical, or overwhelming and must be carefully phrased to be as objective as possible. Above all it should take place under control, deliberately and always in a situation where sufficient support is deemed to exist.

2 When recognition has been established or created then it becomes necessary to establish acceptance of consequence. This is based upon the fact that often there is no clear connection in a member's mind between the action he or she performs and the consequences of it. This strategy then is directed to linking behaviour with consequence.

Example

One member of a group had spent quite a large part of the group's session explaining or rather describing problems she had with a mentally handicapped child who was hyperactive. During the course of which, several times she had asked for help and/or support from the other members of the group who were parents and professional workers, either directly or indirectly. As soon as she had finished talking another member immediately changed the subject. The leader intervened by asking whether he had heard what had been said. The reply was affirmative. The leader then asked whether he had heard the requests for help. Again the answer was yes. He was then asked what did he think would be the consequences for the mother of the handicapped child of ignoring her requests and immediately talking about something else. The point was eventually established about the 'masked' rejection of this action and also that the group as a whole would in future tend to accept that a request for help would tend to be ignored and thus that there was no point in making them. When asked if this was an outcome he desired from his action, the man was indignant and refuted this suggestion with some heat. 'I did not mean it like that', he said.

The question the leader of this group put to the member was on the lines of 'This is what you did; these are the possible consequences; is this what you wanted to happen?'

3 One other connection needs to be established and that is the one which exists between member abilities and the value and utility they may have for the group.

Example

A newly-arrived member in a learning group became quite depressed by the amount of experience the other members of the group had in common and to which she had access only by report. When asked by the group leader why she did not share her most obvious ability with the group she was most perplexed. She was not aware of any ability that she possessed which the others did not have in abundance. The leader replied:

'Oh, yes! You are new – the others have worked a long time together, they share a common language and a way of looking at what they are doing. You have the ability to introduce a new, unknown viewpoint on their work. You have the ability to help them enormously by being a sounding-board. For instance, if they can explain what they are doing with clarity to you and you can understand, then they can be more sure that they themselves have got a clear grasp of those ideas.'

The group duly used their new member in this way and she became valued and trusted as a member, which continued even when her original ability had decreased with time and familiarity.

Resources

If a group leader asks the group what resources they possess the answer, if there is one, tends to be given in material terms, for example, accommodation, finance, equipment, and so on, which is why direct questioning not correlated to a particular situation is not a very fruitful strategy. There are others, however, which are:

1 The word 'resource', while clearly understood, possesses considerable problems for people who have never clearly thought through what 'resources' they actually possess. Indeed, many people in distressed situations sincerely believe that they are resourceless, powerless and helpless. Thus example and precept form the initial strategy. A simple way into this is to use personal experience and to ask or ascertain what members have learned from it.

Example

A team of professionals had become very depressed by what they saw as a consistently obstructive and unconcerned attitude by their immediate management team. They believed that nothing they attempted could change the system. Directed to discuss personal experiences of previous stultifying management situations in their professional lives, it quickly emerged that at least three had survived such experiences elsewhere. One had found another post but the remaining two had belonged to teams which had found methods, not only of coping, but of changing the situation for the better. The team were inspired to adopt some of those change attempts to their own situation.

This example brings into relief a very important point which is that although resources to cope with a situation may well exist within the group and this may become obvious at some stage, it is by no means certain that the group members who possess the resources will see their relevance to the current situation without prompting. 'Why didn't I think of that?' is a common response when the connection is ultimately established.

2 Resources which relate to a particular situation are much easier to locate, thus a second strategy is to clarify and define needs. 'What help can anyone offer?' is much weaker than 'We need to be able to contact voluntary agencies in this area, so has anyone got connections with, or knowledge of, any of these agencies which we can use to get started?' or it may be a matter of skills. 'We need to be able to present our ideas in an acceptable form. Has anyone any previous experience of doing just that?'

3 When examples of resource-use have occurred within a group, it is imperative that the process should be discussed. This ensures that members of the group have a first-hand awareness of how resources are located and used, and above all what an extensive variety of human experience and ability may constitute a resource. The whole process of the definition of need and of resource allocation or matching should be learned by the group and become one of its own skills.

4 Where opportunities which would demonstrate the resources group members possess do not occur naturally within reasonable time, then situations must be created which will generate the possibility, for example, through role-playing given situations, posing hypothetical but relevant situations, and requiring group members to use their knowledge, understanding and skill to devise methods of coping. It must be possible always for group members to see the relevance of these exercises and care should be taken that whatever they discover about resources available to the group should be strongly and swiftly integrated into the real purpose for which the group exists.

5 Many human resources seem only to emerge when a genuine crisis or need arises. Over a period of time during the life of a group several such situations can arise. Again what emerges must be made carefully visible to all group members and stored in the group's repertoire of available resources. In this way the group comes to know which members of the group can provide which services as individuals or in combination with others or as inspirers of others.

It is almost a truism that the most frequent reason for a group's existence is that in combination its members have potential and actual resources available far in excess of those possessed by any individual. The groupworker's problems are:

(a) to define and locate them,
(b) help members to realize their worth and free them to offer resources to fellow members,
(c) help the group to use these resources which are thus made available in a productive way.

Status

1 **Identification of high status members**   Identifying features are as follows:

  (a) Members who possess known positions which are accorded status by society at large and the group members in particular.
  (b) Members who have apparent and demonstrated skills.
  (c) Members who form the basis of subgroups, because they offer protection, support, understanding.
  (d) Members who present behaviour patterns known to be associated with high status, for example, they are able to deviate from group norms without the application of sanctions; they are in receipt of far more communications from their peers within the group than they pass on to others; they are the source of more new and different ideas than others and sometimes they have certain charismatic qualities.

2 **Identification is essential,** because high status group members have the potential to be some of the group's best assets. Recognition must be followed by a process which is designed to integrate them firmly into the group. This is often best done by a public ceremony of recognition of what they have to offer and by the gift of some key roles within the group's structure. This strategy also has to have as one of its main supports a clear recognition that high status members need rewards for their contribution to the group as much as any other member.

Example

A team formed from several different professions found that after a year of existence they were no closer in their working relationships than when they started. In fact the only thing that defined them as a team was their meeting to discuss work allocation. The problem appeared to reside in the fact that each member of the team had remained within the professional identity and status accorded him/her by their own particular world. On examination it was discovered that each knew relatively little about the roles and abilities of the others. An exercise was performed under the guidance of an external trainer, which consisted of each team member writing his/her name and a brief description of their professional and team roles on a wall chart. These were then displayed on the walls and the team circulated the room writing their understanding of person and role underneath. A group session followed with each member presenting and discussing and questioning what was on his/her chart. The discrepancies in perception which were exposed led to a resolution by the high status members to make a much greater effort to adapt themselves and their resources to the different milieu of the team as they perceived the team would thus be more attractive.

3 **Esteem**   One of the main deterrents to the absorption of high status members into a group lies with their perceived loss of esteem. The accepted strategy in this case has to show that esteem related to professional status is not threatened by acquiring a different kind of esteem as a valued member of a group or a team. The anxiety is often based upon a lack of understanding of the role of a group or team member which can be alleviated by discussion and experience and acceptable example.

Example

A team which had been functioning reasonably well for eighteen months acquired a new member who had been part of a similar team in a different part of the country which had been functioning for some years. The team felt almost shy about the amount of experience and development they had achieved and accorded a very high status to their new member. For his part he was not at all happy about the level of competence of his new colleagues and withdrew to what amounted to an observer/commentator role as he assumed that this was necessary to protect not only his self-esteem but also himself from over-involvement. The team resented this development which they saw as diminishing access to what could have been a valued resource. Unfortunately the situation was not resolved because no neutral assistance was brought in and the situation was eventually terminated by the transfer of the new member elsewhere in the system at his own request.

A4 Aims and goals

Definition and comment

Members of groups who have not been compelled to attend by some authority which they either respect or cannot refuse to obey, usually have in mind that joining a group will produce benefits for them, which, as far as they are aware, they cannot achieve in isolation either at all or in satisfactory measure. Groups are established to achieve a goal or set of objectives which may be as narrow as one single situation or as wide as general social interaction. Leaders and organizations create and run groups for purposes which coincide with the policies of those organizations. Thus it is possible for even a small group to find a plethora of aims and objectives held by individuals for themselves, for other groups, and organizations, and for these in turn to have goals for everyone else as well as themselves. These multiple objectives need neither be held in constancy nor with the same degree of intensity at different times and they are also subject to change as factors within the group and those outside which bear on group function also do not remain static. So within a group there are many interests and expectations many of which will be similar and/or over-lap, some which will be in different degrees of conflict and some which will be mutually exclusive. It is well nigh impossible that this maze of interest should ever be fully exposed because, for one thing, the process of exposure causes it to change. What can be achieved is to make visible and known those interests which are consonant with, or which are at least not antagonistic to, the general agreed purpose of the group, and also to make visible those which would seriously impede its progress. Dangers and impediments which are known can be avoided, allowed for, encompassed – those which exist but are unknown remain dangers.

Examples of problems

'We created an "operational policy" for the team almost before the team was formed. It does not now seem to bear much relationship to the everyday aims we seem to be working to.'

'Groups can be set up to legitimize what has already been decided.'

'How do I deal adequately with the achievement of personal goals within an organization with different aims?'

'I would like to know what are the basic aims and objectives in groupwork.'

'How can I translate my concern for my clients into appropriate group goals?'

'How do I allow freedom of interpretation while keeping to group aims?'

'I find it difficult to strike a balance between the individual needs of group members and the overall task of the group.'

'The aim of this group was to encourage personal growth and development, social skills and employment seeking. The actual management of this group left me wondering whether it could have been improved.'

'How do I find an appropriate starting point which adequately sets out the goals of the group?'

'How do I learn to define the aims of the group more clearly?'

'The aims and purposes of a carefully handled discussion amongst a group of offenders about their offending need careful planning and definition.'

'I have a problem of setting appropriate aims and objectives for clients of a social-work agency – matching my expectations to theirs while still provid-ing a medium for growth and learning.'

Analysis of problems

The problems here reflect the traditional concern of goals within a group. Thus there are a number of possibilities:

Probable target of unit goals		Member (individual)	Other group member	Group leader(s)	Subgroup	Whole group	Containing system	Other outside interests
Participating units having goals	Member	√	√	√	√	√	√	√
	Leader(s)	√	√	√	√	√	√	√
	Subgroup		√	√	√	√	√	√
	Organization	√	√	√	√	√	√	√

The probable complex of aims and goals within a group possesses many possibilities of partial conflict or incompatibility; there is the added complication that exists, that of the open or hidden nature of these goals. There are even what might be called 'subgoals', that is, only partially recognized expectations. Finally, there are changes in goals as a group progresses or as the circumstances of members, in or out of the group, change.

Useful ideas

Cost/reward   Whatever the goals of a group may be, personal, group or organizational, unless each member achieves some level of satisfaction from attending the group which is higher than his/her perceived costs (and given that attendance is not compulsory), then he/she will cease to attend either physically or psychologically.

Consensus   This is not held to mean total agreement, but a defined area of agreement which directly concerns the group's function. It is developed as the common ground which all members will accept and may be changed, added to or decreased by negotiation. This often forms the basis of a group contract.

Commitment   In a sense this is similar to costs and rewards. A group is an energy system and it functions on the commitment of energy from members. Essentially giving up some personal aims or delaying their achievement in favour of others which are more group-oriented will only take place on the basis of assuming that a more or less equal satisfaction is available, or on taking a rational or moral decision to do so, for example, to care for or assist others.

Hidden agenda

Usually aims which individual group members hope to achieve for themselves or even for others or the group and to which they commit energy and behaviour, but which have never been made explicit to the group. They are always there and they often bring about group behaviour which is relatively inexplicable, as well as diverting what would be available energy away from the central group goal. In most groups, group leaders may well be the possessors of a large hidden agenda which, with the skill they exercise, could well become a large part of the group's overall goals.

Operational policy

This usually comprises 'designer' aims for a group established by the organization in which the group is embedded. They seem to have one major problem which is that they are created almost in a vacuum and usually before the group to which they refer has actually come into existence. Provided that when the group or team is formed it has the freedom to restate the policy within certain parameters then this problem is soluble.

Clarification

There is a great need for all goals to have an acceptable degree of clarity – the consequence of not ensuring that this exists is that some members, honestly believing that they are working towards agreed goals, will, because of difference of interpretation, be doing something quite different to others and usually wholly unware of it.

Change/renegotiation

Goals formed and stated at the beginning of a group may need serious revision later because the group may well have learned from their sharing experiences that the original aims are no longer adequate. This new understanding should form the basis of renegotiation, for example, it may have become clear that the original goals were negotiated in some ignorance of the time, resources, abilities, and so on, available and should now be restated in terms of the new reality.

Strategies

Pre-group interview

A very simple and obvious strategy in the establishment of goals, aims and purposes in a group is the pre-group interview. It has several values:

1 It enables the group convenor to begin to formulate ideas of how prospective group members think and feel about it:

   (a) The problem or difficulty which is the probable reason for the creation of a group.
   (b) Actually becoming a member of a group and, more importantly, what their level of knowledge and experience of group membership is.
   (c) How these revelations actually square with the assumptions made by the convenor about the necessity for and the kind of group required.

2 It begins a relationship between the group convenor and the prospective member which may be one of the few factors that all members will hold in common.
3 It will probably serve to indicate suitability for the proposed group and may also indicate that other modalities of service may be preferable for some interviewees.
4 It elicits the degree of interest or otherwise of the prospective member.
5 It compels the convenor to clarify his/her ideas about the group in order to be able to present them effectively.
6 It may highlight problems like availability, like transport and other essentially practical factors.
7 It probably forms the basic understanding of what and where to start and the essential ground rules which will be needed to get the group off the ground.

Contract

This idea, now well covered in groupwork literature, is probably a basic approach to some of the problems connected with the aims and goals of a group.

Prerequisites:
1 Some degree of clarity about the purposes for which the group has been created. I know that this looks like a phenomenal act of begging the question but the emphasis is on the processes of exposure and clarification. There are probably as many conceptions of the aims of a group as there are members and they may all be legitimate, but they do need to be made visible at least as far as is possible in the atmosphere of the early stages of a group. So ask the group members, spend some time talking about expectations.
2 To know as far as possible what is on offer. This is difficult because even experienced groupworkers shy away from the question 'What have you got to offer?' So, it becomes essential to be able to state with simple clarity what

skills, knowledge and experience the groupworker brings to the group, because this then can act as a template and a guide to the other group members in expressing what they have to offer.

First contract This is in effect an agreement based in the state of knowledge available at the time about:

(a) the long- and short-term aims of the group;
(b) its simple rules of procedure;
(c) simple clarification of some major roles;
(d) statement of the known resources;
(e) simple rules of behaviour; and
(f) a promise to renegotiate at any time when the original agreement appears to be inadequate in the face of the group's development.

The crucial point is that the 'contract/agreement' can only be negotiated in the light of the available knowledge. One-sided contracts assume ignorance on the part of one of the major contractors, usually the group members, and are often associated with essentially directive group leadership. But even such a contract creates a map for the journey and, even if the route is chosen by the leader without reference to the members, there is some sense that the process of entering and working with a group has some known parameters.

Many group members may need help in coming to terms with their part of such an agreement. It should be given freely and as far as possible in an unbiased way.

The form of such contracts can range from simple verbal agreements to fairly complex written documents. In any event the essential aims and goals of the group may well change over time either in focus or general nature and this should be recognized, made known and the contractual agreement changed in keeping.

Filter

A strategy which is essentially a form of selection which takes place after the initial gathering together of prospective group members, is the filter. This exercise is most effective where a large population of 'suitable' group candidates exists. The steps are as follows:

1 The basic design of group which will be used to meet a known demand or need is made.
2 Prospective members are canvassed.
3 They are all then asked to attend several large group meetings where the basic aims are:

(a) to get to know the prospective members in a situation which is significantly different to those in which they would normally operate and much closer to an actual working group milieu;

(b) to filter those most appropriate, on the evidence of these sessions, to take places in the working group;
(c) if more than one group is available to select again on the basis of observation, a combination of prospective members which will apparently facilitate, probably in different ways, the basic aims of the proposed group;
(d) propose other kinds of attention, if it is deemed appropriate, for those not integrated into the group or groups.

This process can also be used in a smaller group by designating the first 3 to 4 sessions as a filter. This allows members to get the feel of being in a group, the leader(s) to note particulars of the blend of members which is available. Again those who do not continue past this probationary period, must be offered alternatives if this is deemed appropriate.

A word of warning. Wherever any form of filter system is used it *must be made expressly clear that the group proper starts when filtering has been completed. It is not sufficient just to tell prospective members that this is so, but feedback must be obtained that they have understood what is involved.*

Clarification

It must be recognized that even if prospective members and members in the initial stages of group formation are well informed, either with verbal or written material or both, it is not adequate to assume that they have identical forms of understanding of what is involved. So the process of clarification of expectations about the purposes of the group, of the leader, of the individual and of any organization which encompasses the group, should be continuous and thorough. It is also obvious that the degree to which people will divulge with absolute sincerity their ideas about why they attend, or what they expect, will vary enormously with such a large number of influencing factors, that statements can only be accepted as valid for that particular stage of the group life. Conformity behaviour will often obscure real motives, but clarification exercises will frequently generate comments which indicate a growing trust and a greater ability to state matters which were previously hidden.

Verbal clarification – quite simply asking group members what are their expectations. This is wholly appropriate if and when a member's behaviour or statements have indicated that he/she appears to be operating to a different kind or degree of purpose to the others.

Written clarification – various ways of approaching this exist. For example, by a direct request to write down what the aims of the group are perceived as being and comparing the results. Indirectly it is possible to ask members to write down how far they see the aims of the group as being achieved. A common indirect method is to draw the group's attention to redesign. Thus after it has been in operation for some time the group would be asked 'If we were starting this group from the beginning how would you set it up?'

It is not beyond the bounds of groupworker ingenuity to design many such approaches, but it must be realized that the approaches are not the salient business. They are but methods used to refine, clarify and ultimately to form a consensual core of group behaviour.

Example

A group of entrants to a social work course were given, during the three days of a residential induction, information about each other, the course, the staff, the material and structure of the course itself and various other bits of information. This material was presented in several different forms which included feedback, written work, verbal work, and video material. Four weeks into the course students were asked to discuss the clarity of the course objectives. The result indicated such differences that the students could have been deemed to be attending different courses. A considerable number of what had been puzzling responses to the course up to that point, now were shown as stemming from widely disparate expectations. Indeed the expectations that students had held when first arriving at the course in all their degrees of difference appeared to have been reinforced by the induction material rather than to have modified or clarified them.

Essentially, clarification requires that feedback should indicate quite clearly what kind of understanding has taken place. Indeed, I often have cause to think that the question 'Have you understood that?', which ultimately can be answered by a simple 'Yes' or 'No', is a pointless exercise. A request which requires a statement, for example, 'Please tell me what you have understood by that', serves to elicit the nature of the understanding which is then available for comparison and the beginning of a common understanding. Which leads directly to the next strategy which is concerned with the development of consensus.

Consensus

Total agreement is an ideal state. The basis of the strategy of consensus formation is to create a visible operating base which is founded on those areas of credible agreement. If, for instance, we can represent each member of the group in terms of his/her aims, purposes and expectations which they bring with them into the group as a circle, then diagrammatically those areas of the circles which overlap represent those parts of the members' aims which have been made visible and agreed.

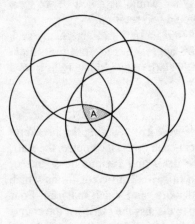

Diagram 1 5 group members, probably in the early stages of a group . . . the shaded area A represents the known consensus and agreement, and can serve as the basis of a working contract.

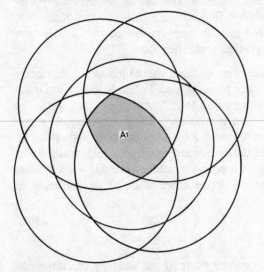

Diagram 2 5 group members at a later stage in the group's development. There is now a much larger exposure of members' aims and a larger area of consensus. This area, A1, is also proportionally a larger part of each member's aims.

The essentials of the development of consensus can be listed briefly:

1 The need to establish a rule or norm of appropriate disclosure.
2 The need to create space, time and support where required for every member to make their contribution.

3 Where verbal ability is not a great strength, the need to use other forms of contribution, for example, written, diagrammatic, dramatic, and so on.
4 To isolate and make clearly visible the areas of positive agreement.
5 To indicate those areas in which partial agreement already exists.
6 To decide into which areas expanded agreement should go in the future.
7 To use the consensus area as a basis of a working contract, renegotiable later.

Example

A working group had many widely different attitudes to the exercise of leadership within confines ranging from an acceptance that directive leadership was an essential fact for the group to other members who believed equally strongly that the group was merely an organizational structural element. As professional equals they were agreed only on one thing, that the service they provided was hindered by this large area of disagreement. It was decided that they must establish procedural rules which they described as a compromise. This was done by each member writing down what he/she would accept, what he/she would not accept; an attempt to define within what limits each would find it possible to make a working compromise and a commitment to discuss openly and to bide by a majority decision. What emerged was a fairly complex arrangement which could be briefly described as an allocation of different parts of leadership responsibility to different members. No one member had overall control but each had a designated responsibility, all of which was renegotiable under given circumstances and in any case at six-monthly intervals or at any time when new directives arrived from the employing agencies. The consensus was based on the areas of actual and probable agreement.

Acceptance of difference

Difference which does not initiate fear or prejudice is the basis of much of the resources which a group possesses. Indeed, where the group has been convened on the basis of similarity of problem, the differences in the way in which individual members have attempted to cope with it when made available to each other can demonstrate possibilities of coping heretofore unthought of by others. Thus the strategy of the promotion of the acceptance of difference rests upon a very firm base. In essence it relies upon the technique of the demonstration of value. But it must be clear that the value demonstrated should be one which the group not only accepts but also believes to be of worth to them. Many examples of the use of this strategy are given in this text but one more will not, I hope, come amiss.

Example

In a workshop devoted to the problems of groupworkers one of the members was an administrator in the local authority social services department and a groupworker with a voluntary organization in his spare time. As all the other participants were full-time professionals, this difference, admitted on the first day of the workshop, persisted by hint and innuendo for several days and caused the administrator to reduce his exposure to the group, until they began to discuss the shortage of material resources, sports equipment, people with special skills, knowledge, and so on. Hesitantly the administrator offered the fact that he possessed access to a considerable amount of information about such matters, indeed he had access to a recently made inventory of local resources which he was quite prepared to share. The group, on some gentle prodding from the workshop leader, explored their response to difference and in particular the way that the administrator had been treated and were led to explore what change, if any, had taken place in their attitudes when that difference proved to be a potential asset of some magnitude.

Perhaps the greatest block to the acceptance of difference occurs when the differences involved are the subject of strong stereotyping and/or prejudice. As both these influences tend to be generalized to populations or types, the basis of dealing with them must be the urgent recognition that people are individuals and unique even though they are also members of a class, a type or category.

PRESENTATION OF PROBLEMS CATEGORY B

B1 Performance and behaviour

Definition and comment

What is visible in a group or team is the behaviour of its members. Its performance, which is not so easily accessible, is the measure of how successful it is at achieving the tasks it has set for itself. This is too simple, of course, and has to include the way in which it conducts its business, deals with situations and the level of attraction that it develops for its members. Seldom do practitioners mention the performance of a group until that performance is either significantly good or obviously poor. But the performance of individual members within the group is a much more visible situation. However, there is still a hidden problem. A bravura performance by an individual must not be judged so much as a performance in its own right, but almost entirely on the consequences it entails for the performer and for the group. Thus a great demonstration of the growth of insight by one member may be wholly appropriate both for the member and for the group, acting as a catalyst to other members who were unsure of how to express what they felt. The same performance may in different circumstances be highly destructive in overawing unprepared members and leaving the performing member hurt by their lack of response and thus being driven back into self-concealment. Commonly behaviour within a group is assessed on the basis of its value to member and group either in terms of furthering aims, in maintaining the group and the individual in good working and emotionally viable order, or in providing an element of necessary security.

Examples of problems

'There are power struggles within the group.'

'Some members are so dominating that it is very difficult to deal with without undermining their confidence.'

'How does one deal with disruptive incidents within a group – does one encourage members to be loyal to the group whilst feeling free to act out their difficulties?'

'There are problems with relationships within the group and the need to perform particular duties – the group is encouraged to be responsible for planning performance.'

'Some members seem incapable of keeping group confidences.'

'The use of avoidance as a blocking technique acquired over a "career".'

'Dependency on and within the group . . .'

'How to cope with the turnover of membership – some are constantly dropping-out and being replaced, which inhibits the group – continuity and cohesion are lost.'

'In this adolescent residential unit scapegoating is a particular and frequent group problem.'

'How to cope with a group member's refusal to participate in discussion especially when her disruptive behaviour interferes with the effective working of the group?'

'How do I handle group members dropping-out and the effect that this will have on the group – to minimize negative effects and maximize any positives?'

Analysis of problems

In this batch of common problems there are five major categories of member behaviour all of which relate to disturbance of the group functioning, namely, power conflicts, disruptive behaviour, responsibility issues, attendance problems and the ubiquitous procedure of scapegoating.

The first four appear to have been noted solely because they impede the smooth or efficient working of the group. But scapegoating, although presented in this way as destructive, is traditionally seen in groupwork literature as a maintenance gambit. From a practical point of view it may be difficult to believe that something so cruel and hurtful as scapegoating can have any positive values. But I think that such is the case and in particular the value that it has in common to the other forms of behaviour as well – namely that they are all indicative of the ways in which the group and/or individual members are dealing with arising situations within the group *as they see them*. In this sense it is essential that the strategies designed to cope with these particular behaviours should be based on some real understanding of the purposes the behaviours are designed for or used to achieve. Which is why, as we shall see, the terms used to describe such behaviours have to be stripped of their pejorative connotations right at the beginning. There are very few people whose main pleasure in life is to respond to all situations in a 'bloody-minded' way. Such behaviour may be a well-developed technique which has been found to be successful in achieving personal ends in the past but that is a different thing from the concept of the deliberately destructive and disruptive person.

Useful ideas

Group functioning   There is a basic assumption that the behaviours listed are those which interfere with the smooth functioning of the group hence the statement of them as 'problems'. But it is well to be cautious, particularly in circumstances which produce power struggles, disruption, scapegoating, dependency, and so on, that these manifestations are not so much 'problems' but responses which, given the developmental stage the group has reached, its composition, its task and other pertinent factors, are wholly or partially appropriate. It often seems to me that the observer bias (discussed elsewhere in this book), which predicates a strong tendency to describe behaviour as stemming from the personality traits of the 'actor(s)', is creating an imbalance of understanding in relation to the idea that such behaviour is a response to the situation as the 'actor' sees it. Conflict, challenge, withdrawal and blaming others are all essential parts of everyday existence and whereas their presence in a small group increases their visibility enormously, this is no reason to believe that they stem from 'bloody-minded' members whose enjoyment comes from causing severe disruption. Fortunately such people are very rare. Thus it is more logical to assume that the responses listed above are *responses to* a situation.

Power   The ability to influence in a desired way the behaviour of others. When members feel safe to attempt the exercise of power it may be threatening to others but it is likely that it marks a stage in the development of the group as a unit.

Conflict

Conflict implies the discharge of energy and may be necessary in order to clear the air and in allowing the energy to be used more productively.

Disruption

Some 'disruptive' behaviour is remarkably successful in drawing attention to the disruptors. Most workers in residential situations are aware that often a disproportionate amount of time is spent with those residents who have a high nuisance value. But 'disruption' may be wholly legitimate as a way of bringing aspects of the group situation to notice, to change course, to challenge, to make a personal statement, even to find out how 'disruption' is dealt with. Groups have to establish the safety margins and this is best done by some form of 'testing-out'.

Open groups

Most groups are in fact 'open' in the sense that membership of any session is not necessarily identical with the last. Drop-outs, intermittent attenders, just emphasize the effects which are described in the literature as pertaining to 'open' groups, for example, the formation of subgroups, the need for structure, reduction in the intensity of relationships, level of commitment, and so on. If such changing membership is inevitable then the design of the group and its aims should be made in full cognizance of what such behaviour can and will impose.

Holding

Part of the design for a group must contain some appreciation of the need to make it attractive enough to 'hold' members at least until they have had sufficient experience of it to know what it has to offer currently and in the future to its members.

Scapegoating

There is a wide literature on this phenomenon which makes very interesting group reading. In groupwork it is usually used to describe the situation in which one or two members of a group become the focus of the group's dislike and bad feelings. There are several major points which can be briefly stated:

(a) Some people seem to expect to become the focus for abuse and dislike in groups.
(b) Some scapegoats are chosen by groups on the basis of very visible difference.
(c) Scapegoating may be a maintenance technique which allows the group to stay together.

(d) It may also be used to excoriate those members who are seen by their peers delaying their development and progress.

(e) The group leader may need to take the role of scapegoat during periods of particular group need, for example, when a group is winding down.

Apparent non-participation

This is quite a common statement and one which has to be met by the question 'How do you define participation?' Most usually it is by reference to production of the major group activity. But it is more than likely that some group members have little confidence in their ability in the major group activity, for example, talking, but given that deficiency are participant at another level. This does not mean that such members should not be encouraged to develop some facility in the prime group activity, but it does mean that care should be taken before they are taken to task for not 'participating'. As will be stated frequently here, everyone expects that it is necessary to learn how to handle a car, for instance, it is no less necessary that people learn how to operate in a group.

Prejudice

Briefly this is an attitude or belief directed at or against an individual person or group of persons to which certain characteristics are attributed and which causes, supports or justifies discrimination on the part of the attitude holders. It may be one of the 'funding' motivations in the process of scapegoating.

Strategies

Power conflicts

The first part of any attempt to cope with power conflicts is to relate what is occurring to the developmental sequence of the group and the events which it is facing.

Power conflicts are *natural* occurrences when:

1 The group has been together long enough to feel secure enough to challenge the designated power structure.
2 When a subgroup containing high-status group members wishes to bring about change of structure, purpose or direction.
3 When there is blatant dissatisfaction with the existing power/control structure and the success of the group is of great importance to its members.
4 When members feel that their sense of self-esteem is under threat.
5 In the early stages of group development when the group appears to be exposed to an external threat.

6 When a closed group is coming to the end of its term of existence.

Usually power conflicts are the result of certain group members believing that such challenge is essential if ends which they hold dear, either for themselves or for the group, are under threat or are not being achieved. Thus the second part of any coping strategy must be to make the consequences of the behaviour in question visible. This must not take the form of a threat or it becomes self-defeating, but should lucidly and clearly spell out the probable outcomes. This should then be followed by the question, 'Is this what you are seeking to achieve?' If the answer is 'Yes', then for the security of the group it may be necessary to accept the outcome, but to attempt to discover some different and more group-friendly way of achieving it.

If the answer is 'No', then it becomes necessary to discover what the aim was in the members' terms and once again to pursue the possibility of devising an acceptable method of achieving it, providing that it is legitimate individually and/or in the interests of the group.

Example

The natural leader of a group in a residential establishment was discharged and his position within the group taken by another. After several weeks the original group leader was readmitted to the same establishment and within no time at all challenged the current group leader. However, things had changed considerably during his absence and most of the group were quite satisfied with the situation as it was. With one or two supporters the old leader created an extremely destructive struggle for power, by a process of challenge, undermining the current leader and appeals to past successes. Staff at the establishment became obliged to convene a meeting of the group and to point out that the group comprised mainly members who had either not known the first leader or only slightly, that they had been together long enough to regard the older leader's challenge as a threat to the group which caused an increase in bonding and resistance. It was agreed that the challenge arose from the simple fact that the old leader had never considered that there would be any problem to his resuming where he had left off when discharged. The solution was to move him to a different section of the establishment where he clearly understood that his knowledge and experience could be of value and in which he might well be able to create a leadership role for himself if he so wished as the group he was about to enter had no strong cohesion, no obvious leader.

Essentially the power of individual members in a group may be controlled by limiting the number of communications they receive, monitor and exchange with other members. When conflict between members occurs then their strength resides in the reinforcement their behaviour receives from other members. Reduction of this power base may often result in reducing the conflict to directly manageable proportions.

Conflict resolution and conflict management

The difference between resolution and management in conflict strategy is quite simply that between conflict which ceases to exist because its energizing factors have been dealt with, and conflict which continues but in controlled form – to use current jargon it becomes a 'damage limitation' exercise.

A fairly comprehensive survey of techniques involved in these two major forms of conflict strategy can be found in Douglas (1986: 175–83) but additional material is available here.

In 1970 Blake and Moreton developed a managerial grid which had as its vertical axis 'concern for people' and for its horizontal axis 'concern for production results'. Thus conflict management strategies are related to the dominance of either of these concerns thus:

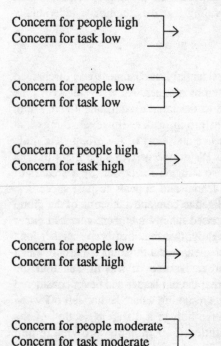

Concern for people high
Concern for task low → Conflicts are smoothed or ignored – the appearance of harmony and a peaceful co-existence is maintained.

Concern for people low
Concern for task low → Neutrality is stoutly maintained – no effort is made to deal with the situation – barriers are erected.

Concern for people high
Concern for task high → Viable problem-solving occurs based on the evaluation of different points of view – it is fact-centred, emotionally restrained – doubts are examined and worked on.

Concern for people low
Concern for task high → Authoritarian suppression of conflict – power struggles are fought to win or lose positions – sometimes involves outside arbitrators.

Concern for people moderate
Concern for task moderate → Compromise – no winners or losers – solutions are accepted which are 'workable' rather than 'best possible'.

This substantiates groupwork practice in that time-limited, clear task groups, with known resources, tend to need a high level of directive control, whereas groups with much longer spans of available time and with personal growth goals and unknown potential resources need a much more facilitative and nurturing approach.

However, it is clear that attempts at conflict management and resolution must be adapted, not only to the stage of group development, but also according to the degree of task or group-growth orientation present at the time.

Frey (1979) warned that there were two major obstacles to conflict resolution or management:

(a) Conflict blindness – responses which are 'tramlined', for example, habitual.
(b) Choices made on the basis of impulse.

Strategies are therefore aimed at reducing 'conflict blindness' and helping to create a degree of choice over response patterns.

Frey lists eight processes which may help in this way:

1 Building and establishing trust.
2 Developing and building personal strengths.
3 Increasing the degree of accuracy of communications (both in sending and receiving).
4 Determining the validity of assumptions.
5 Establishing what the individual goal might be and how similar/dissimilar it is to those of others.
6 Establishing that there are alternatives to prevent 'tramlining'.
7 Selecting alternatives by an examination of consequences.
8 Planning how selected alternatives can be put into practice.

Most of these are long-term strategies, but when implemented they do tend to reduce the pressure towards further conflict.

Frey also lists several techniques of conflict resolution/management which I will give here briefly:

1 Ask members to list and chart previous conflicts and their outcomes. This will probably make visible habitual patterns and styles of conflict resolution.
2 Play games which depict a conflict – role play – simulation.
3 Chart unresolved conflicts – in discussion such charts should serve to indicate areas of conflict blindness and also suggest alternative coping strategies.
4 Use video, role play, socio-drama to get acceptable alternatives in place as part of the individual's coping strategy.

For strategies for coping with *disruptive behaviour* which could be extremely relevant in this section, the reader is referred to the extensive coverage given in Chapter 6, example B on pp. 144–9, where it is dealt with as a leadership problem.

Responsibility issues

There are two basic issues here:

1 The responsibility that the group has for the group itself.
2 The responsibility of the members to and for a group.

The basic strategy for the group leader includes the necessity to define clearly different responsibilities according to the needs of the group at separate stages in its life. But what must concern us briefly now is when the assumption of responsibility is counter-productive.

In essence this occurs when a developing group sees a conflict between the stated policy of the group being the instrument of decision-making and the group leader assuming sole responsibility for important decisions.

The responsibility of members for what occurs in their group is inextricably linked with their individual perception of the value that the group offers them. Thus all strategies in the creation of member responsibility are concerned with generating rewards for membership that are 'real' rewards in the terms that members would use to define them or potential or deferred rewards which are available and can be worked for. Rewards may exist in many areas of human experience, for example, a member may be proud of his/her membership and of the group's achievement – highly involved and in demand, happy to be with compatible people, and so on. Within the constraints in existence and the parameters of a group design, it is not beyond the bounds of reality to effect the development of member responsibility by devising methods which bind members to their group in appropriate ways. If this is not done, as the following example shows, responsibility will remain with those who have demonstrated the willingness to accept it.

Example

A groupworker running what appeared to be a 'good' group was faced with the problem of splitting the group because of administrative changes in his organization. But however much he tried to facilitate the group to decide on the nature of the split, the members would not make any decision. Individually they had expressed opinions, but within the group they always 'talked-out' decision sessions. A later review of the group's long existence revealed that in fact the members had never been offered, much less taken, responsibility for major decisions. They had no expectation of a right in this area, only in making minor and incidental decisions.

Attendance problems

Opting-out and failure to attend are a common manifestation of member responsibility or rather the lack of it. This is not a criticism of such activities but to indicate that responsible behaviour *vis-à-vis* a group is largely a product of the level of satisfaction that a member gains from his/her membership. Thus strategies must start from a series of questions:

1 Is the absence of a given member 'legitimate' in his/her terms, that is, is the effort of coming not worth expending, or is it a response of fear, a comment on the group, and so on?

2 What effort has been put into holding the group together long enough for potential rewards to emerge?

3 Have all avenues been explored which would increase members' understanding of what the group has to offer in terms they not only understand but accept as real? The relevance which is obvious to people who create groups is not always either so relevant or so obvious or even important to potential group members.

4 If one of the principal energizers of the learning process is interest then it is equally true about group membership. Is the group interested?

I have given no technique here for a very simple reason. What needs to be done depends so much on existing circumstances and upon the answers to the four questions noted above.

Scapegoating

The characteristics of this problem as usually defined in groupwork are two: the act of laying-off on to one member of the group the blame for whatever is currently going badly for the group, and there are certain kinds of people who are selected by groups to receive this blame.

Therefore strategies are equally two-centred – to deal with the scapegoating behaviour and its consequences, and to help those who appear 'marked' to be the scapegoats. The strategies presented here will cover both aspects.

The first point in forming a strategy is to realize that the group member is inevitably selected as scapegoat on the basis of perceived difference, for example:

(a) in social power – usually low – believed to be unable to retaliate;

(b) possesses obvious characteristics which incur notice and probably dislike, for example, physical characteristics, manner, speech patterns, provocative behaviour, and so on. It can be almost anything though it is always something which appears as a 'difference' to other members whether or not it also incurs dislike;

(c) an apparent acceptance of being put upon which is demonstrated by repeatedly placing him/her self in contact with persons and situations which are injurious and shows no evidence of adaptive learning in this situation. In fact he/she often appears to intensify potentially dangerous situations. This appears to be provocative and entails attack, the scapegoat attacks in return, and points to being attacked as the reason for retaliation. All this he/she seems to recognize as 'bad' but also to be out of his/her ability to control. In other words it is a circular response.

The first action is to make visible and known to all the group what is happening and to point to the possible consequences. The consequences are important for very often scapegoating behaviour is hidden under the guise of a 'bit of harmless fun'. What belies this is its consistency and frequency both of occurrence and in selection of victim.

The second action is an act of clarification. This means spelling out to the group the basic reasons for scapegoating behaviour. In essence these are: that it is a serious, often intuitive, attempt to keep the group in existence by depositing bad feelings which are inhibiting, on to one person. In this sense it is a positive group action and this must be stressed.

Third action is to point to the cost. The group is being saved by victimizing one person.

Fourth action is to show that a similar maintenance effect can be achieved in other ways without the cost of individual victimization. These ways include making the maintenance problem visible to the group as a whole; taking collective responsibility for it and sharing the decision about group resources to be allocated to dealing with it. There may be some mileage in the group leader accepting the role of scapegoat on a contracted and transient basis to allow the group time to reformulate their approach. Garland and Kolodny (1966) listed twelve techniques for dealing with the problem of scapegoating as follows:

1 Squashing the behaviour, using the power and authority of the leader position.
2 By careful selection of group members so as to avoid choosing members with potential scapegoat behaviour patterns.

Neither of these is recommended procedure, especially (2), largely because the information levels about potential members are inadequate to make such a selection and in any case it is unjustifiably arbitrary.

3 Talk about what is happening – an excellent idea.
4 Protect the scapegoat – this may well be very necessary in the early stages but as a prolonged strategy it has unwelcome consequences and something more positive than using the leader's position as a protective shield should be substituted as soon as practicable.
5 Create a diversion – a very stop-gap measure.
6 Reduce interaction – likewise a temporary measure.
7 Strengthen the scapegoat – this is usually done by making him/her aware of and begin to understand their behaviour and those factors which have led to their selection for the victim role. An attempt must be made to rebut the victim's assertions that the process is out of his/her control.
8 Clarify the process of scapegoating – this is essential anyway for the scape-goating response is seldom a wholly conscious manoeuvre on the part of group members and such clarification is a precursor to:

9 Focusing in the group on the scapegoating process which in turn could lead
   to:
10 Engaging the group in the process of controlling the scapegoating.

Personally I find the idea of attempting to control the process to be far less
effective than attempting to discover alternative processes, less damaging to
individuals. After all, scapegoating arises because a group has some need to discharge ill-feeling, frustration, anger, and so on, and controlling merely displaces
the energy involved on to other, probably equally damaging, methods of
coping.

11 Role play – simulation, socio-drama, role play – are all methods of making
   visible the actual process of scapegoating and of bringing home at the level
   of experience to those involved what it is all about and the kind of consequences which can ensue. They are all part of the process of clarification
   which is so essential in dealing with any problem. But they can also be used
   to construct alternative methods of coping with the group's needs which
   have been met by the scapegoating process. In this sense the role play can
   be a planning exercise, 'If we try to do this what will it be like?' When
   some idea has been achieved then to simulate the situation design can give
   useful practice before attempting to integrate the designed behaviour into
   the actual group.
12 The final strategy is removal from the group. This can take the form of (a)
   removal of the scapegoat from the group, (b) the closing down of the group.

(a) is not recommended except in extreme necessity to protect the victim. Most
evidence points to the fact that removal of the 'victim', the focal part of the
process which has as its main function the relief and maintenance of the group,
without tackling that group need by the provision of some other process of
relief, merely initiates the selection of another scapegoat.

The second form (b) must be based upon an admission that attempts at
substitution have failed and that the costs of the group's continued existence are
too high and unacceptable.

It must be realized that prejudice and dislike are often amongst the basic
drives in the selection of a scapegoat and that conscious aims, that is, to hurt
and to humiliate for reasons almost wholly unassociated with the group's
existence, may be present. The evasion of responsibility for behaviour lies at
the base of much blaming of others as well as a credible belief that others are,
or may be, actually at fault. But the essential fact that scapegoating is often a
group maintenance process must not blind groupworkers to its costs nor to the
fact that, in so far as it may solve one group problem, it almost invariably
entails others.

There is a very large literature on this process for indeed it has always been
an extremely common form of behaviour, often possessing ritual and mystic

significance. A brief selection of that literature is appended here in the references at the end of this chapter.

B2 Roles

Definition and comment

A role is a social function carried out by an individual. It tends to be limited by
rules and presents certain opportunities. In another sense it is a pattern of
expected behaviour reinforced by sanctions which limit an individual's freedom
of expression.

Much has been made of the 'natural' roles that people play within groups, but
very little of the fact, in groupwork at least, that members of a group can be
taught and learn to perform certain crucial roles within the group for which no
'natural' performer is available.

With the 'natural' roles, the recognition that they exist must wait on their performance by individuals within the group with a degree of frequency of
occurrence which serves to make reasonably sound the assumption that the performers have a propensity to behave in this way. Roles which are thus seen to
be beneficial in that they move forward the achievement of the group will be
encouraged, developed and used appropriately; roles which run counter to
group development will be diverted, changed or brought to a halt if possible.

It may well be that from experience it is known that certain well-established
roles are an essential prerequisite of group functioning. In this case a leader
may well select certain suitable members and coach them in the function
pertaining to these essential roles to ensure the healthy development of good
group functioning. Finally it must be remembered that 'role' is a term which is
a description of a particular kind of behaviour – roles as such do not happen in
the sense that they do in say drama – role is a short-hand and functionally
effective and accepted description of a behavioural figure (see pp. 95–7 for
constellation of roles functioning as a 'role structure').

Examples of problems

'Some members have been around so long that they consider themselves to
be experts by right of tenure.'

'Some members seem to set up patterns of confrontation and conflict wherever they are.'

'There are several roles I find difficult to cope with, for example, the waffler,
the sniggerer, the dismissive and those who think the group is a dumping
ground for their every problem.'

'I find the uncooperative member difficult.'

'There are others who have great difficulty in joining in, raising some issues on the degree of persuasion that might be required.'

'Those who insist in making all their communications directly to the leader.'

'The disruptive member.'

'There are problems relating to a power struggle between the oldest established couple and myself as a nearly new worker in post.'

'There are members who volunteer for tasks but never carry them out.'

'The professional victim who says, "Everybody's always getting at me".'

Analysis of problems

As would be expected, in the member roles which have been noted as problems are those which either challenge the leader's concept of his/her role, or those which are seen to frustrate the progress of the group. Thus roles which are noted are essentially similar to behaviour (see previous section), which is noted and for basically the same reasons. The difference lies simply in the concepts of frequency and of expectations. What has been described as say 'disruptive' behaviour may be a phenomenon of relatively short duration. If it is not, but becomes the expected and produced behaviour, of a group member in particular circumstances, predictable, frequent and similar, then in every sense of the word it has become a 'role', a part, which others in the group have every reason to expect will be played when the cue is given.

The 'professional victim' is in essence a scapegoat. It is interesting that scapegoating is seen as member behaviour but being a scapegoat is seen as taking on a role (see previous section).

Whatever roles people take on they have to have the basic and most fundamental aspect that they deliver to the performer some level of gratification in some area of his/her existence even though others may totally fail to discover what it might be, though occasionally people occupy roles trapped by the expectations of others.

Useful ideas

Role performance   Once again there is a large literature on roles which should be consulted – but it should never be forgotten that the concept of role is a description, a convenient way of referring to a pattern of behaviour. Indeed many 'role performers' are basically unaware that their behaviour can be seen as a kind of 'dramatic' act. Others are wholly aware that they are 'playing a part', usually because they have found it successful in similar circumstances in the past, and/or it gives them satisfaction, or they are involved in 'image projection'. Leaders may need to ponder this carefully, for they often are 'performers' acting the part of a group leader based on what they deem necessary for the group. The fact that they are very visible adds point to this because the nature and quality of that performance may set a standard for others to follow – the leader becomes a *role model*.

Role entrapment   A very delicate point this for a lot of groupworkers who find it hard to accept that they have been cast in a particular role or set of roles by their group members which does not conform to the role they have set for themselves. It is possible to change the perceptions which underlie this casting but it should be remembered that group members can find themselves 'trapped' in a role from which they can see no way of escape, for example, 'I feel they always expect me to smooth things out and I find myself doing just that even when I don't really want to'.

Role structure   A way of looking at the relationships which exist between the roles which members play (see 'role structure' in 'Group Problems', Chapter 6, pp. 95–7).

Strategies

Role demonstration

Where roles which are essential to group progress are weakly played or not forthcoming at all, then it is feasible to use strategies which develop in willing members these roles:

1 A simple method of starting this process is for group members to compile a list as individuals of those skills, behaviours and contributions which they deem to be necessary for the stage which the group has achieved. In discussion of the lists it can be ascertained how many of these requirements are already present, present but underused, or not demonstrably present at all.
2 The next stage is to devise the roles required in terms of their essentials and initiate members into their performance by role enactment, and role-modelling, video presentation, and so on.

Example

A subgroup of a large working group set up to perform a series of tasks had been allocated a time-limited task which involved information collection, discussion and decision-making regarding priorities. They had been instructed that they would need a directive, controlling leader and an efficient recorder. The leader was quickly forthcoming but no one in the subgroup knew precisely how the recorder would work. The leader then indicated that in order that their work together should not be diminished by inefficient recording they should spend the early part of their time creating, informing and in essence training the kind of recorder that their task demanded. The time was well spent and the group was well satisfied that their efforts were truly presented to the main group with minimal loss.

Perhaps the most interesting spin-off from this experience was the effect of deciding that the skills required of their recorder and going through a pooled, though brief training session, would have on the cohesion of this particular group and the enhancement of their ability to work well together. Demonstration, within the group, of how things can work, has a powerful effect on members' perception of the group's use and value. They may have often been told that this was the case, but until they actually see it happen, such instruction has only a marginal effect, unless it can be related to experience. People seem much more able to believe what they experience directly rather than by being informed verbally:

Strategies for clarifying and making visible the roles within a group

1 **The first and most important aspect of these strategies is that the group members should not only understand what they are about but that they should also consent to the exercises involved** – thus the first approach is to discuss the roles members perform in the group within the parameter of overall safety which the group can provide. Two questions are of value here: 'How do I affect the group?' and 'How does the group affect me?' In the process of discussing these and in receiving feedback from his/her peers, each member can gain insight into the relationship between their behaviour and the group's performance.

2 **Role analysis** – this can be accomplished in many different ways, for example, by role-playing, interviewing each other, using rating scales, filling wall-charts on each other and so on. But perhaps the most useful form is for each member of the group to provide a written commentary on the roles played by all group members including him/herself. Each member then receives the comments from all the others which he/she can then compare with his/her own analysis of their role. If the comments are identified as to their origin increased learning can take place by asking questions to clarify the comments. There are, however, certain advisable rules to be followed in the employment of this strategy:

   (a) Role analysis should only be attempted when the group has been in existence for some time and members have had an opportunity to observe each other.

(b) It should usually be done when the supportive nature of the group is adequate and when, apart from the apparent need to clarify and make visible roles within the group, there is little other strong pressure on the group.

(c) Feedback should always be soundly based on observed behaviour and not in speculative or interpretative comment.

(d) Judgemental behaviour is out, but linking behaviour to consequence is in.

(e) Each member should speak for him or herself – while others may not agree that their observations coincide with another's, a personal statement of perception must be accepted as a true report.

In essence these are *ground rules* for attempting an exercise and more about such rules will be found in the next section under 'Norms'.

3 **Demonstration of consequence** – one of the simplest ways of promoting knowledge and understanding of the effect of roles, is to take examples from current experience and trace in discussion the implementation of role behaviour and the sequence of events, feelings, and so on, which could be agreed were dependent upon them.

Example

A group which had a poor record of observing its own agreed ground rules consented to the appointment of one of their members as a kind of watch-dog. Over a period of time during which the watch-dog intervened, was shouted at, agreed with, resented, encouraged, and so on, the leader suggested that it might be useful to look at the effects on the group of his appointment. When they realized how little they had used the watch-dog role latterly they were able to assess that they had integrated the ground rules to their behaviour patterns and no longer spent so much time arguing about structure and devoted more time to the group's essential task. Indeed they agreed some of the ground rules were now so accepted that no one could question them.

(Refer to Chapter 4 (pp. 82–8) on 'Norms' for extra information about *ground rules* and *modelling* and *role consequence, reinforcement* and *reassignment* in the same chapter.)

DISCUSSION

Members, their abilities, experience, background, aims, behaviour, roles, problems, contacts, not only comprise the group in physical terms but they are also the source of energy and of the resources with which the group will work. The totality of the group resource system is bounded only by what the group, that is, the members and leaders together, can provide or develop. At one end of the spectrum there are highly-skilled, knowledgeable group leaders who provide a large part of the group's resource system; at the other there are equally skilled and knowledgeable group leaders who labour to create a group in which the members learn to use their own resources by a process of exposing what is available and by pooling their discoveries. This latter group leader then becomes only one of several resource systems which are available to the group.

Perhaps the most difficult of these areas which relates to the beginning of a group must be the quality of the information about members which is available. This is one reason why directive group leadership may be so readily attempted in that the leader has a greater level of knowledge about the resources which he/she possesses in these early stages. It is also why the factor of time is so important. If the resources of the group are to be used then sufficient time must be allowed and an appropriate situation generated in which these resources can be allowed to emerge and be made visible and eventually used. This leads directly to the problem of holding the group long enough for this to happen. Difficult as it is, this process of holding, that is, keeping and developing interest and commitment in the group, produces a much better group eventually than a precipitous attempt to make the group work unless, of course, the group is essentially dependent, and will remain so, upon the resources of the directive leader.

What must emerge from even a cursory consideration of the problems discussed in this chapter is that a shift of thinking is necessary in working with groups, away from the individualistic and highly personal process of daily life to the consideration of being part of a functioning unit. There is an ever present need to realize very clearly that part of one's consciousness of being is allocated to the unit of the group and to define that part which remains undisclosed and personal. I suppose in an indirect way this commitment, this realization that in some areas the group and its interests should come first is really the raw energy which actuates the system which is the group.

One last point is that all group leaders need very specifically to understand that the personal worlds of group members may be similar but they are not identical. Which should lead to a direct consideration of the meaning of behaviour patterns for those who produce them every bit as much as to a consideration of the general consequences of those patterns on the group. For example, the term 'disruptive' behaviour implies a viewpoint of a behaviour pattern which is located in concern about its consequences for the group and therefore invites responses which are aimed at dealing with those consequences. It does, therefore, unbalance the response which ought also to be concerned with the personal aims of the individual using that behaviour. Safety of the group may well be of paramount importance and should be effectively maintained, but it is not necessarily an automatic choice and the loss of precious group resources may cry out for a different solution.

SECTIONAL REFERENCES

A1

Benson, J. F. (1987) *Working More Creatively with Groups*, London, Tavistock Publications (Selection, pp. 25–7; Tolerance of Difference, p.124).

D'Augelli, A. R., Chinsky, J. M. and Getter, H. (1974) 'The effect of group composition and duration on sensitivity training', *Small Group Behavior* 5(1): 56–64, London, Sage Publications.

Garvin, C. D. (1981) *Contemporary Groupwork*, Englewood Cliffs, NJ, Prentice-Hall (Composition, pp. 68–78, 82–3).

Gruen, W. (1979) 'Energy in group therapy: implications for the therapist of energy transformation and generation as a negentropic system', *Small Group Behavior* 10(1): 23–39, London, Sage Publications.

McGrath, J. and Altman, I. (1966) *Small Group Research*, New York, Holt Rinehart and Winston.

Shalinsky, W. (1969) 'Group composition as an element of social group-work practice', *Social Service Review* 43(1): 42, 49.

Stava, L. J. and Bednar, R. L. (1979) 'Process and outcome in encounter groups: the effects of group composition', *Small Group Behavior* 10(2): 200–13, London, Sage Publications.

Tuckman, B. W. (1967) 'Group composition and group performance of structured and unstructured tasks', *Journal of Experimental Social Psychology* 3: 25–40.

Vraa, C. W. (1974) 'Emotional climate as a function of group composition', *Small Group Behavior* 5(1): 105–20, London, Sage Publications.

Woods, M. and Melnick, J. (1979) 'A review of group therapy selection criteria', *Small Group Behavior* 10(2): 155–75, London, Sage Publications.

A2

Benson, J. F. (1987) Ibid. (Trust, pp. 94–7, 139–40; Trust Games, pp. 50–6).

Garvin, C. D. (1981) Ibid. (Techniques for Changing Members' Affects, Cognitions, Perceptions, pp. 153–5).

Goodman, D. W., Randolph, D. L. and Brown, H. J. D. (1978) 'Attitudinal group-centred counselling: effects on openmindedness', *Small Group Behavior* 9(3): 403–8, London, Sage Publications.

Hartford, M. E. (1971) *Groups in Social Work*, New York, Columbia University Press, 119.

A3

An excellent reference covering:

(a) The change mechanism in groups.
(b) Areas where groupwork is the method of choice.
(c) What kind of clients will benefit.
(d) Contra-indicated client problems and categories.

will be found in:

Northen, H. (1987) 'Selection of groups as the preferred modality of practice', in J. Lassner, K. Powell and E. Finnegan (eds) *Social Group Work: Competence and Values in Practice*, New York, The Haworth Press.

Wilcox, J. and Mitchell, J. (1977) 'Effects of group acceptance/rejection on self-esteem levels of individual group members in a task-oriented problem-solving group interaction', *Small Group Behavior* 8(2): 160–78, London, Sage Publications.

A4

Contract

Benson, J. F. (1987) Ibid. (Worker/Group Contract, pp. 46–8; Worker/Client Contract, pp. 96–100).
Douglas, T. (1979) *Group Processes in Social Work: A Theoretical Synthesis*, Chichester, John Wiley and Sons (Contract Formation, pp. 93–4).
Garvin, C. D. (1981) Ibid. (Types of Contract and their Relation to the Stages of Group Development, pp. 101–2).
Maluccio, A. N. and Marlow, W. D. (1974) 'The case for contract', *Social Work* (January): 28–36.

B1

Benson, J. F. (1987) Ibid. (Aggression/Challenge, pp. 80–1, 121; Domination, pp. 195–6; Responsibility, pp. 110–15, 177–9).
Blanchard, P. D. (1975) 'Small group analysis and the study of school board conflict: an inter-disciplinary approach', *Small Group Behavior* 6(2): 229–37, London, Sage Publications.
Cowger, C. D. (1979) 'Conflict and conflict management in working with groups', *Social Work with Groups* 2(4): 309–20, New York, The Haworth Press.
Dentler, R. A. and Erikson, K. T. (1959) 'The function of deviance in groups', *Social Problems* VII(2): 98–107.
Garvin, C. D. (1981) Ibid. (Deviance, pp. 71, 76, 99, 171, 257).
Genthner, R. W. and Falkenberg, V. (1977) 'Changes in personal responsibility as a function of interpersonal skills training', *Small Group Behavior* 8(4): 533–9, London, Sage Publications.
Horwitz, G. (1968) 'Worker intervention in response to deviant behavior', unpublished PhD thesis, University of Chicago (December).
Pawlak, E. J. and Vassil, T. V. (1986) 'Restructuring cooperation among acting-out youth', *Social Work with Groups* 3(1): 31–40, New York, The Haworth Press.
Ross, L. H. and Allan, R. M. (1975) 'Two statistical approaches to two types of group confrontation', *Small Group Behavior* 6(2): 220–8, London, Sage Publications.
Schopler, J. (1965) 'Social power', in L. Berkowitz (ed.) *Advances in Experimental Psychology*, vol. 2, New York and London, Academic Press, 177–218.
Wahrman, R. (1977) 'Status, deviance, sanctions and group discussion', *Small Group Behavior* 8(2): 147–68, London, Sage Publications.
Wodarski, J. S., Feldman, R. A. and Pedi, J.S. (1976) 'The reduction of anti-social behavior in ten-, eleven-, and twelve-year-old boys participating in a recreation center', *Small Group Behavior* 7(2): 183–96, London, Sage Publications.

Conflict

Blake, R. R. and Moreton, J. S. (1970) 'The fifth achievement', *Journal of Applied Behavioral Science* 6: 413–26.
Douglas, T. (1986) *Group Living*, London, Tavistock Publications, 175–83 (there are several references here).

Frey, D. E. (1979) 'Understanding and managing conflict', in S. Eisenberg and L. E. Paterson (eds) *Helping Clients with Special Concerns*, Chicago, Rand McNally College Publishing.

Scapegoating

Berkowitz, L. and Green, J. A. (1965) 'The stimulus qualities of the scapegoat', in A. Yates (ed.) *Frustration and Conflict*, New York, Van Nostrand (discusses those qualities of the potential scapegoat which stimulate aggression).

Feder, B. and Ronall, R. (eds) (1980) *Beyond the Hot Seat: Gestalt Approaches to Group*, New York, Brunner/Mazel, 19 Union Square (Elaine Kepner, role-taking behaviour – 'what is being avoided by having someone in the group act-out a part of themselves', p. 21; Susan M. Campbell, the 'family scapegoat process', pp. 78–9; Ruth Ronall, on 'outsider roles', for example, scapegoat, p. 197).

Feldman, R. A. (1969) 'Group integration: intense interpersonal dislike and social groupwork intervention', *Social Work* 14(3): 30–39 (dislike as a social factor).

Feldman, R. A. and Wodarski, J. S. (1975) *Contemporary Approaches to Group Treatment*, London, Jossey-Bass (the danger of scapegoating as a control and sanctioning procedure during the phase of building a viable and cohesive group, p.43).

Garland, J. A. and Kolodny, R. L. (1966) 'Characteristics and resolution of scapegoating', in S. Bernstein (ed.) *Explorations in Group Work*, National Conference of Social Workers.

Garvin, C. D. (1981) Ibid. (Description of scapegoats as 'overactive deviants', p. 99; Discusses attempts to prevent scapegoats being 'locked into role', p. 123).

Heap, K. (1977) *Group Theory for Social Workers: An Introduction*, Oxford, Pergamon Press (Group success allows members to reward a scapegoat, p. 143. Discussion of scapegoating with examples, pp. 155–63).

Heap, K. (1985) *The Practice of Social Work With Groups: A Systematic Approach*, National Institute, Social Services Library, no 49, London, Allen and Unwin (The diagnostic implications of scapegoating with examples, pp. 95–7; Groupworkers dealing with an episode of scapegoating by (a) general discussion, (b) understanding the group's anxiety, (c) confrontation by pointing out the value of the scapegoat's statements, and finally (d) by looking at the strengths and weaknesses of both sides in the process, pp. 102–3).

Mann, R. D. (1967) *Interpersonal Styles and Group Development*, New York, John Wiley and Sons, 186–95 (Suggests that all resisters may be scapegoated – puts forward the thesis of the 'sexual' scapegoat).

Shulman, L. (1967) 'Scapegoats, groupworkers and pre-emptive intervention', *Social Work* 12(2): 37–43.

Chapter 4

Problems relating to the group as a system

GENERAL AREA OF PROBLEM

Although a loose collection of individuals produces behaviour patterns which are identical with those of a 'created' group in some stages of its development, it is not a 'group' in the sense that most of the presenters of the problems discussed here would recognize, but probably the essential factor in this difference may be only the duration of the association.

When a group is created, that is over a period of time, and efforts have been made to lay down a structure or structures with a programme, it may eventually be in a state where it can function as a unit/system in its own right.

It is the problems which arise in the process of creating that function, but more particularly those that occur as a result of that system functioning, which are dealt with here. Once more the offered problems seem to divide easily into two main categories:

A   Those problems which arise from the structural properties or nature of the group, for example, its subsystems like its role structure, power structure, and so on
B   Those problems which arise directly from the nature and quality of the group's performance as a system.

Under category A group problems have been presented in the following subcategories:

A1   Normative structure.
A2   Subgroup structure.
A3   The open or closed nature of the group.
A4   Role structure.

Category B contains only those problems of assessment of group progress:

B1   Measurement of change.

It is interesting to note here that the apparent perception of the intrinsically systemic nature of a group is not widespread. The concept of 'groupness' is only available to those who have learned to see the patterns which a constellation of individuals interacting over a period of time can form. Thus only the more obvious concepts of group structure rate as a 'common' problem.

A1 Normative structure

Definition and comment

The normative structure of a group can be defined as the set or sets of rules, obligations and standards by which the group operates, and which is generally accepted by all group members.

Changes are effected usually by consensus or by majority agreement, or even in some cases by imposition. Perhaps the most interesting factor about normative behaviour within a group is where the standards come from. In many instances, where rules of behaviour are not made explicit, the general behavioural patterns of the culture from which the majority of the group members come seem to be followed within the group almost without question. This poses several interesting questions, namely, if general social rules prove to be inadequate for the task which the group has in hand, then before more appropriate rules can be agreed it is often necessary to make explicit the norms which have been operating up to the point of change. Again, when group members do not all come from the same or even similar cultural backgrounds, then the rule systems they will follow are different and there is thus even greater necessity to make an explicit normative structure by agreement. What passes for disruptive and destructive behaviour may often be produced by group members operating to a different set of learned rules from others within the group. Such non-visible differences may also be the cause of both psychological and/or physical withdrawal from the group through a lack of understanding of the rules by which the group appears to operate.

It is to be noted that establishing a set of norms which is wholly appropriate to the reasons for which the group exists is one of the more useful tools to facilitate effective group performance. But it should also be noted that the greater the difference between that group set of norms, and those of the larger systems of which it is a part, the greater the need for a careful realignment of members when returning to or operating in the larger systems.

Examples of problems

'What kind of ground rules can we establish in the group?'

'I've heard a lot about contract – how do I make a contract with my group members and how do I get it implemented?'

'How do we establish a group which is cohesive and safe?'

'If honesty and trust are so important in the group, how can they be established?'

'How can we establish as a norm of the group that members should obtain adequate levels of satisfaction from attending?'

'There seems to be a great need to enable the group to understand its own structures.'

'How do I get a group to establish its own identity and to impress upon residents that the group meetings are for their own use rather than being an organ of staff control?'

'When a member uses all the time available for a session to talk about a traumatic relationship and obviously needs support, should the group leaders break the contract agreed between members and leaders in terms of the time allocated for each session?'

Analysis of problems

All human systems, large or small, have to be regulated by rules, however few, so that everyone knows how important areas of maintenance behaviour should be performed. But most human systems also change over time and there is a need for the rules governing behaviour to change also. This places the necessity of deciding by key members of the system, which rules should be adhered to and which need to be changed. So all the problems in this particular set reduce to two extremely basic factors:

1 Appropriate rules or norms of behaviour and how to establish them.
2 What are the appropriate or acceptable levels of conformity to norms already established?

It is axiomatic that a group cannot function at even minimal levels of efficiency if it has not established a consensual agreement about its basic procedures. The problem of the newcomer to an established group highlights the difficulties of members who do not know the rules, which is why induction processes are of such great value in enabling such new members to find their place in what can present as an alien society. It should also be remembered that although some degree of conformity is an essential prerequisite of effective functioning there are other options open to members in dealing with the pressure a group can exert: compliance, internalization, identification, co-operation and competition.

Useful ideas

Norms   These are basically *ideas*; held at an individual level by
                     members of a group about what should or should not be

done in specific circumstances by the group and its members. They are *not behaviour*, but they define the limits of acceptable behaviour. They form the basis of control within the group – when they develop in the early days of a group they are extraordinarily resistant to change – there are formal norms, explicitly-stated norms, non-explicit informal norms, and unconscious norms – they cover liking, control, decision-making, status, acceptance, achievement, success, and so on, as well as behaviour.

Sanctions   Wherever there is a rule governing behaviour there is also some form of punishment, be it only disapproval, for those who do not conform without acceptable excuse or reason. Ostracism, direct reprimand, all the way to expulsion and sometimes physical and verbal violence are all forms of sanctions applied to inappropriate behaviour.

Ground rules   In essence a simple form of contract indicating those areas of behaviour which are acceptable and those which are not. This is making the basic norms of the group explicit. They are often propounded in the early stages of a group by a leader based on his/her experience of what serves to create the beginnings of a group with the emphasis on safety and holding.

Contract   A more formal set of rules which includes short- and long-term aims for the group, expectations and definition of contributions. Like the ground rules, contracts should contain the explicitly stated intention of renegotiation as the group changes and develops and as greater clarity and understanding of what is possible is arrived at.

Newcomers   New members arriving in an established group have always been a focus of interest because they serve to highlight the difference between member and non-member in respect of possessing a knowledge of, and working within, the accepted procedural norms. The presence of a newcomer invites a review of those norms, clarification and the production of an induction process to facilitate the newcomer's integration.

Conformity   There are many ways in which members adapt to group norms (see analysis in this section), but perhaps the two most important ways for the groupworker to know about are (i) public conformity and (ii) private acceptance:

(i) public conformity is fundamentally a ploy for maintaining personal safety by an individual inside the system which in his/her estimation is too powerful to challenge and which demands specific behavioural forms. The correct behaviour patterns are produced and maintained only as long as the system is perceived to be monitoring them – when this ceases the individual's behaviour tends to revert and little or nothing of the conforming behaviour remains;

(ii) private acceptance occurs when the individual not only wishes to change in the way that the system requires, but is also aware that it is possible, reasonably safe and desirable. Such changes as are made remain in some form or other when the individual is no longer in the group or the change system. In a way the change becomes personal and permanent.

Consensual core   This is the idea that members of a group will agree to accept a minimal core of rules for the group's behaviour for the sake of beginning to get the group off the ground although they may not be wholly convinced. It can be the beginning of the balance of individual commitment being tipped away from personal need to the needs of the group as a unit.

Strategies

1 Making ground rules

Making ground rules at the beginning of the life of a group is an effective way of covering basic aspects of security, acceptable behaviour, methods of working and so on. In essence it is the beginning of the formation of a set of norms for a particular group and situation. Many groups attempt to create a mini-society in which the rules are significantly different to those of the larger society in which the group exists. The reasons for this are quite simple and are usually contained within the idea of developing a milieu which is supportive rather than indifferent or even hostile. But the essential point is that such systems take time to develop because often the rules are so different from those to which members have been accustomed that they have to become convinced that their adoption is to their benefit.

Example

A group of civil servants working with a trainer from a different background were involved in a five-day workshop on social behaviour. The ground rules which were adopted on the first day covered such matters as taking responsibility for one's own learning, freedom to question and all the usual security and sincerity statements of such a learning situation. But the level of personal commitment within the group remained poor, each member was carefully guarded and very selective in his/her responses. Eventually there emerged two points which experience of working with this kind of member would have shown to be of great importance in the quality and sincerity of their response. The first was that members were from different grades within the service, and the second, that a reporting system was in existence whereby senior grades were expected to file reports on the work and behaviour of junior grades.

New ground rules were quickly formulated which stated that the workshop was a learning situation and was not subject to civil service rules, there would be no reporting back, and that the problem of the presence of different grades was to be part of the workshop study. This led to some very interesting exchanges and the emergence and acceptance of the human beings who occupied certain positions within the service.

Ground rules should therefore have two very simple components:

1 The need to take notice of the particular anxieties of members which might inhibit their productive involvement in co-operation within the group.
2 That they should be made with the whole-hearted agreement of the group's members, but also in such a way that they are understood and can be seen to link directly to their knowledge of what is going on.

Ground rules should be used as markers to enable members to feel that they have some signposts to guide them in the way that they are going. (A good example of ground rules established for group therapy is to be found in 'An experiential approach to group therapy', in R. C. Diedrich and H. A. Dye (eds) (1972) *Group Procedures, Purposes, Processes and Outcomes*, Chapter 17: 219–27.)

Of course, where rules exist, there is some need to have sanctions which may be applied to transgressors. It is very easy to find many references to rules and norms in groupwork literature, but extremely hard to find even an indirect reference to sanctions for non-conformity. However, it must be remembered that sanctions are, or can be, positive and rewarding just as easily as they are negative and punitive.

2 The application of sanctions

The ultimate sanction for refusal to conform to the rules agreed by the group is expulsion from it, but the use of this particular sanction must be limited to two major forms of non-conformity:

(a) when the behaviour in question threatens either the total existence of the group or so diminishes the benefit to other members that disintegration is a very probable consequence, or
(b) when the behaviour of the non-conformer is such that his/her safety and existence within the group is no longer viable. It is well to remember that

where groups can take the decision to apply such a sanction by virtue of possessing the requisite knowledge and understanding of what is involved, it should be a group majority decision. There are occasions, however, when the group leader(s) may, by virtue of extra experience and understanding, have to take such responsibility – the group, being in such a state, being unable to do so.

Positive sanctions such as reward, encouragement, support, the giving of responsibility, and so on, are methods of demonstrating that conformity to a group's agreed rules, confers benefits and sets an example for others to follow.

Negative sanctions such as the withdrawal of support, verbal criticism, temporary ostracism, removal of responsibility, confrontation including demonstration of the consequences of behaviour, are also models of behaviour and become part of the ethos and culture of the group.

Example

A group of social workers in a groupwork training workshop had rules governing the attention that each member should give to the utterances and behaviour of others. One member, however, became so enthusiastic about a line of thought he was pursuing that as other members who were struggling to enlist the understanding of their colleagues with their problems paused in their statements for comment, he would immediately continue with his monologue. As several opportunities for discussion were lost in this way the anger of the group grew. Eventually the leader cut across the inconsiderate member each time he butted in. After this had occurred several times the leader brought the group to consider what had been happening. The inconsiderate member was not only informed about the consequences of his behaviour, he had experienced them. When this was clear, his enthusiasm was acknowledged, space was created for him to express his ideas, and the opportunity was also created for the other members. The sanction of 'experience of consequence' created a much closer observance of the rules of procedure.

It is advisable that sanctions should be part of the rules with which any group starts its life. It may even be possible to define sanctions which the group as a whole would apply and those which, at least initially, should be applied by the leader(s). It is axiomatic that the beginning of norm-formation and the use of sanctions to encourage such a process should start very early in the life of a group. There is evidence which would indicate that norms which arise and are accepted in the formation stage of a group are extraordinarily durable.

3 Modelling

In essence this is an implied sanction in that the leader, or other, models the response pattern which is appropriate to the group rules and which can then not only stand as a demonstration but can also be compared with the non-conforming behaviour of other members.

4 Discussion

As non-conforming behaviour, especially by high status members in a group, is often the precursor of change, it is advisable that before sanctions are applied full and frank discussion of the non-conforming behaviour and its possible consequences should take place. It is worth repeating at this point that most important consequences of social intervention are most often totally unforeseen – which gives some leeway for risks to be taken within the boundaries of the group's capabilities.

5 Effect of behaviour

In the process of applying sanctions it must be recognized that any verbal procedure will have far less effect on the observers than the behaviour involved, and method of application. As this is true of all forms of group intervention and will constantly recur, I do not wish to overstate it here.

A2 Subgroup structure

Definition and comment

All groups are part of a larger system and are themselves containers of smaller systems. Because we are here interested in the group as the basic unit then the smaller systems a group contains are usually referred to as subgroups. Group research has indicated that subgroups are frequently the focus of change within the group and in this sense they are often opposed to some, if not all, of the system. They are usually combinations of group members who band together for support, because of some readily identifiable similarity or because of an affinity or liking or even because of pre-existing relationships. As will be apparent from the problems offered here, many groupworkers find subgroups threatening and/or problematic. It is perhaps little comfort to point out that the building blocks of any group are the dyadic relationships which exist either permanently or transiently within it. In very blunt terms, a group is a collection of permanent and shifting dyadic relationships. To complain about them is like complaining that trees are full of wood.

Examples of problems

'How do I deal with unintentional (from my point of view) subgroups?'

'There are wheels within wheels – wheeling and dealing by subgroups.'

'In my groups there are stable patterns of subgroups – usually based on the need for support.'

'What are the stages of development/evolution of subgroups?'

Analysis of problems

There is clear recognition that subgroups affect the way in which a group works. What seems to be being requested is further understanding of how and why subgroups form and more information on how they may be worked with. Some slight appreciation of the power of subgroups is apparent, and in particular the phraseology used to describe them would indicate that they can be a frustrating phenomenon. Subgroups are alliances of members usually founded on the basis of some common interest; they may be long term and durable, or transient, serving the purpose of the moment. But, whatever form they take, they possess all the potential of being combinations of power, support and may be either reactive or initiating. Fundamentally, as all large groups are essentially configurations of smaller groups, it can be argued quite convincingly that any group with which we work is a partly stable, partly fluid combination of isolates, dyads and triads.

Useful ideas

Subgroup formation   Usually takes place around group members who discover over time that they have common values, attitudes and interests – around personal attraction or repulsion – friendship – previous relationships – around the discovery of complementary needs which may be transient or permanent.

Originating ideas   Subgroups are frequently the source of new ideas and initiatives which are able to move the group as a whole in a different direction, when this is positive, that is, compatible with group aims, it is good; but subgroups can also be negative, destructive and deviant.

Collusion   In order to achieve certain ends members can form power cliques to exert pressure on the rest of the group. These subgroup power bases are usually temporary but also frequently lead to the promotion of other coalitions brought about by the repayment of indebtedness located in the bargaining that created a power base in the first instance.

Nature   Some theorists argue that the basic building blocks of all groups are three: the individual, the pair and the triad, and that all larger groupings are constellations of ones, twos and threes, in which the linkages are to be found in common purpose, interest but, more importantly, in structures brought about by individuals having membership in several of these minor groupings at the same time. Where subgroups congregate physically multiple membership implies a choice of attendance which may well be dictated by indebtedness or current interest. But the degree of attention which any one person can give to others simultaneously may be the major natural predisposing factor in the ubiquitous formation of minor groupings (see, for instance, Darrell Smith's (1978) article on dyads).

Pairing   This is probably the commonest form of subgrouping and tends to occur as a mutual support system – it is the basic interactive system.

Strategies

All strategies for working with subgroups have to take into consideration several basic factors about the group:

(a) The stage of development which the group has achieved.
(b) The legitimacy of the subgroup, in terms of the major group's aims.
(c) Their relationship to systems external to the group.
(d) Subgroupings in existence prior to the group.
(e) The nature of the subgroup.

1 Identification

Subgroups are identified on the basis of the following observable characteristics:

(a) The popularity of an individual member who becomes the central focus. This may be a one-way system towards the central person.
(b) The reciprocity of the individuals involved at (a), thus the subgroup proper comprises those people who are mutually attracted to each other whether it be on the basis of liking, respect, security or whatever.
(c) The intensity of the relationship is also important.
(d) The duration of the relationship is important.

Thus strategy 1 recognition (identification) is based upon observation and in reality is a counting exercise so that group recordings are an essential activity.

A point of interest is that some subgroups have a permanent or near-permanent structure, others appear transient. It is important to be able to recognize these differences because their effects are notoriously different, for example:

pairing – often transient – tends to run counter to movement towards group cohesiveness – characteristics are a supportive exclusiveness which may develop into isolation.

cliques – often power-related and again frequently deviant to the main thrust of group development – usually centred round one dominant individual who is in conflict with group norms or the leader or both – tends to foster disorganization.

mutual subgrouping – usually supportive of group morale and cohesiveness.

2 After recognition a decision is required about the legitimacy of the subgroup *vis-à-vis* the group's objectives and well-being.

In the early and termination stages of a group's life the appearance of subgroupings is essentially a security gambit. Until members can have reasonable assurance that the group is 'safe' they will adhere to smaller units of security based on similarity or previous knowledge. This is wholly legitimate and essential. Depending on the degree of cohesion and trust, the group realistically needs to complete its task, so to a greater or lesser extent this small unit support system can be left to function or develop into a whole group trust system.

At termination such subgroupings are again a logical and legitimate exercise as the group breaks down into the component entities from which it developed.

During any stage of change and development in the group, subgroups will tend to form. Particularly if issues of control, power and security are involved. Strategies for dealing with these must depend on whether their existence is ultimately of benefit to the group. Thus, cliques which are usually deviant may be of great value, particularly during periods of high group tension or periods of frustration. Change, beneficial change, often comes from group deviants. It is essential to chart the progress of such subgroups and record very carefully the consequences that they produce.

3 There are several techniques for reducing the formation of subgroups:

(a) **Feedback** – this involves using feedback in the group to expose the development of a subgroup. Essentially then, if the group chooses to accept this development, all that can be done is to offer conjecture about possible consequences and allow the subgroup to develop. Part of the learning situation for the group is to see how their decision produces consequences.

(b) **Contract** – if the contract with the group contains some agreement about the formation of subgroups then it can be invoked and either adhered to or renegotiated.

(c) **Commitment** – this is similar to invoking contract but specifically relates to the aims of the group and to exploring the formation of subgroups (in special ways) as being inimical to their achievement if this should be the case.

(d) **Task group formation** – this is a deliberate ploy of creating task groups within the group in furtherance of the group's agreed aims – whose membership cuts right across that of the subgroup whose existence it is desired to terminate.

(e) **Reduction of isolation** – by involving the peripheral members of the group in general activities, and thus increasing the rewards to be gained by being in the group, the total system can begin to counter the influence of subgroups and bring about their gradual absorption into the group.

(f) **Programme adjustment** – can be made which, while not running counter to the group's aims, serves to increase the rewards for loyalty to the group and enhances the sense of unity, for example, some form of joint social activity.

(g) **Role model** – in this strategy the leader(s) sets the pattern of group loyalty – which must be genuine and also, to be acceptable, must be seen to be no light manipulative gesture but one which actually involves some sacrifice and cost.

Garvin (1981) recommends the use within the group of a fish-bowl exercise in which a part of the group, that is, a subgroup, works under the direct observation of the rest of the group and from whom it later obtains feedback, both on the content of its work and on the processes involved.

The aim of all strategies in this area is to connect to the subgroups and to use whatever resources they can offer for the benefit of the total group. It is only when such approaches have proved useless that the processes for diminishing subgroup formation and influence should be tried.

A3 Open or closed structure

Definition and comment

Basically 'open' groups are those in which the group, as a definable unit in its own right and in terms of its essential structures, remains. The people who make up its membership change over a period of time. Thus group members leave and new members come but a sufficient core remains at any moment in which resides the basic culture of the group. Many, if not most, groups have some element of 'openness' about them particularly if they have a specific focus and exist over long periods of time. On the other hand 'closed' groups are defined by having a membership which stays the same throughout the group's life. Termination in a group like this means the complete cessation of the group's existence at a single moment of time. The major factor for considera-tion is that both defined forms are examples of group design. The element of closed/openness promotes differing possibilities within a group, for example, open groups do not develop the same level of intensity of interpersonal relation-ships as those found in closed groups. The other side of this design factor is that often the aims of the group and the constraints imposed upon it by the larger system in which it is embedded, make one or the other, closed or open form, the only one acceptable. For instance, although it is indeed possible to hold groups within a residential institution, most such organizations are open group systems because of their admission and discharge procedures. As we shall see, a problem occurs in either open or closed groups when individual members defy, for whatever reasons, the terms of the group contract, for example, when members of a closed group 'drop out' and when members of open groups refuse to leave and become permanent fixtures. There are many other factors relating to this problem such as how necessary it is to know the length of time members of a closed group need to contract for achieving their aims in the group and whether such a contract should be renegotiable.

Examples of problems

'Members who drop out create the effect of a group that has a constantly changing membership.'

'Open groups have members who stay for different periods of time.'

'When is it important for the group to be a "closed group" and what is the correct way to establish it?'

'I have a problem of working with open groups and yet have the need to offer a programme to a court.'

'How do I end a closed group – isn't there a problem of letting go?'

Analysis of problems

There seems to be more recognition of the probable effects on a group system of a throughput of members. The changing pattern of members present within a group is clearly appreciated, especially when a programme has been devised for a group to serve the needs of some external or interested agency which has as its foundation a developmental sequence. There is an argument that a totally closed group cannot exist except in extraordinary circumstances, for example, a wholly residential community where for long periods of time the members remain within the community, make no contact with anyone else and do not leave, and to which no new members are added, does not detract from the fact that groups with a greater element of 'closedness' actually produce significantly different patterns to those which do not have such elements. The problems seem to lie in knowing what those differences are and in using them in a positive way.

Useful ideas

Different kinds of open group	See, for instance, Michael Henry (1988) who defines three such kinds: 1　Drop in/drop out. 2　Replacement – a leaving member is replaced by a new member keeping the group size roughly the same. 3　The reformed group – in which members of a group contract into a new group which contains some of the members of the original group. This is often referred to as a 'carry-over' group and research tends to show that far from starting from scratch such groups tend to start almost from where the last one left off.
Group development	The development pattern for open groups is significantly different to that normally advanced for closed groups which is related to a continuing sequence for the same constituents. The development of individuals within the open group may be a more appropriate concept.
Advantages/disadvantages	As we shall note later in 'Design' (pp.129–33) the elements of any group, that is, the way it has been put together, the emphasis placed upon these, is to ensure that certain outcomes are more felicitously arrived at. Thus the essential limitation imposed by a closed group produces the effects of defining the number of possible relationships which is static, intensifying them, making members visible, allowing time for the exposure to behaviour necessary for the development of trust and so on. It also has the probability of creating smugness, stagnation and a dearth of new ideas. The advantage of the open group lies in the choice open to each member as to whether he/she will avail him/herself of the group or not and each can more or less

tailor his/her attendance to need. It generates the
possibility of learning about making and breaking
relationships, it usually has a life much longer than
that of a closed group and so on.

Strategies

As part of the preparation for a group try to ensure that the following information is available:

(a) In the setting and system in which the proposed group will exist, is it
possible that either a closed group or an open group can function?
(b) If not, is there any possibility that change can be effected to allow either a
closed or open group to operate?
(c) Which form of group, open or closed, would be most effective for the proposed members and the suggested aims of the group?
(d) If the chosen form is not possible what would be the probable consequences
of attempting to work within the constraints offered?

In order to be able to answer these questions it is essential to have a clear
knowledge of the types of open and closed groups, and the advantages and disadvantages in use. I would suggest that a basic strategy is therefore to read the
available material on these areas and in the light of the knowledge gained make
appropriate decisions.

A4 Role structure

Definition and comment

Roles are those parts which group members seem either to accept for themselves because perhaps they are both familiar and compatible, or have thrust
upon them by circumstances, necessity or the powerful influence of others.
Some roles are quite clear, usually those which are common enough in all
groups and often enough it does not occur to other members to question them
unless they are highlighted in some fashion by personal or group need. But it
has been said that a group is a system and in any system, mechanical or human,
the parts of it must function to supply the purpose for which it was created.
Thus the roles which members provide have to be essentially those roles which
advance the group in its chosen path or which initiate and support development.
Thus groups can be categorized according to the degree to which their members
have developed the necessary roles for the fulfilment of their objectives. Members can, in most instances, offer facility in the performance of many roles,
though a considerable number of human beings are, for many different reasons,
role-impoverished. What is important for the health of a group is not only that it
has all the more necessary roles within its system occupied, but that they should

energize that system in an effective way. There are thus, for any group with more than just a simple need to continue to exist, a series of role structures or constellations which produce the systems and energy needed at given instances of the group's existence to move it in the direction of achieving its expressed goals. In other words, the roles and role energy that members can contribute to a group's performance constitute its major resource. That they exist is indisputable, that they can be recognized, developed and co-ordinated for specific ends by the group is another matter entirely, and one intimately bound up with members' perceptions of the value of their commitment to the group at any particular time. Disinterest, resentment, external interest, lack of need, illness, and so on, can all make for a diminution in active or even passive role enactment. It is also as well at this point to indicate that both roles and their structures have many different degrees of value to groups. The ability to play major parts in any particular scenario can usually only be assessed on the basis of past known performance. It must be obvious that a great deal of role-taking ability may well be concealed if no situation arises in which it can rightly be produced and thus assessed for its quality. The ability to assess such contributions and to weld them into an effective functional resource may well be one of the greatest contributions any group or team leader can make to the construction of a group. But it can take quite a considerable amount of time and sensitivity to achieve.

Examples of problems

'Since this team was created there has been a blurring of our professional roles and now we are no longer sure of them.'

'Our establishment was founded and worked effectively on the basis of our relationship to the director. When he left we realized that our roles and methods of working had been set by him. How can we work without a structure which will serve as we had before?'

'My training taught me to work as a responsible professional. I find it very difficult to understand how other professionals operate. We are only a team in the sense that we work in the same area with the same people.'

'Three volunteers were part of the membership of this group. I feel we omitted to instruct them sufficiently, especially in relation to their roles within the group.'

Analysis of problems

Individual roles within the group or team are often unclear, largely I suspect because no one seems to take responsibility for establishing what they are, apart from those which have been structured formally by the organization. It is not in the least surprising, therefore, that the relationship member-roles have to each other in reinforcing, complementing, conflicting or neutral ways, eludes group members. The resources of group members are often made manifest in the roles they operate and the problem of gaining access to those resources is greatly reduced if they are known and can be appropriately used and skilfully blended for the group's advantage. The problems listed here are all related to the individual who, possessing an individual role or skill bequeathed by training and previous experience, cannot see what others have to offer, and even when he/she can see, does not have much idea how they can be usefully engaged to support and complement one another. This tends to create certain phenomena. The individual tries to take on all the roles he or she can, or more usually they restrict themselves to behaviour which is familiar. In both cases the group or team loses any corporate identity and becomes a collection of individuals operating as individuals within a non-structural definition, which has no other binding nature. This can often be an effective way of working, especially if the free exchange of information arises within the structure – but the essential point is that it is a different kind of role-structure and it should be understood by all those it contains to be what it is and not something else which is not working properly.

Useful ideas (see the ideas listed under 'Roles' on p. 76ff. of Chapter 3).

Strategies

Perhaps the earliest essential strategy is to endeavour to relate the parts members play within the group to the short- and long-term aims of the group. In this sense the leader(s) can offer guidance by having a reasonably clear idea of his/her own role, having carefully considered what they have to offer. This can be fed into the group as information with an indication of how the members can be helped to achieve a similar presentation. It sounds simple but in fact it is not, for the reason that few of us actually consider what parts we play until circumstances, usually some form of crisis, forces us to consider. Thus the procedure follows this kind of sequence:

1 Establish clearly by discussion and feedback the agreed area of the group's main aim.
2 By a similar procedure seek to establish what kind of parts members will need to play in order to make a reasonable attempt to achieve these aims.
3 The leader(s), by offering experience, skill, knowledge, and so on, can then create a role model for the process of discovering what ability to play those parts exist within the group.
4 The process of matching can then take place and the early try-out stages can proceed.
5 The situation can be reviewed in the light of progress made (or not) and both aims and roles re-examined.

If there is a clear perception of the likeness of this procedure to casting parts in a drama production, then that is a correct perception. Indeed in many teams there is the same part allocation which involves competition, lead roles, disappointment and stand-in situations as one would expect to find in the initial casting procedures for a play.

Reinforcement is a common strategy in all areas of work with groups but it is especially necessary in the development of a role structure. Many group members, though possessing more than adequate ability to fill the roles they have taken on, may find the conscious performance of such roles in what is essentially a very visible situation, rather difficult. Thus when they do well even by minimal standards of performance, they should be rewarded, encouraged and reinforced in the successful patterns of behaviour.

The assessment and discussion of consequence is another strategy which is applicable here. Once more it is necessary to realize that the ability to relate action and consequence, particularly if the two are separated by time and by other complexities, is not well developed. Thus the process should take the form of a comparative review. This is sometimes done by half the group compiling a review of a previous position and the other half operating as a distinct subgroup attempt to create a review of the current position. When these two reviews are compared in the full group the consequences of the behaviour of the group and of its decisions tends to become that much clearer and decisions can then be made about their past and continuing value. One factor which tends to emerge in this kind of review process is that certain roles have become redundant, and another may well be that part of the structure of roles has stuck at a performance level which may once have been relevant but is so no longer. Ossifying role structures create stagnating groups – the security may be at a very high level, and the self-satisfaction – but the developmental and achievement levels may be absolutely nil.

After review, reassignment of some roles may be necessary. This has to be done with care in the light of the threat that all such change may involve, and it must therefore contain some element of acceptable compensation for the effort required. One of the most difficult of role reassignments occurs when it is the leader role which ought to change. Groupwork literature and folklore is full of stories of groupworkers who have not clearly recognized that the role they were currently playing was far less relevant to the stage of their group's development than it had been.

Example

In a learning group of groupworkers the leader had pursued a dual role of group leader and tutor in the early stages of the group. Because of their experience the group gelled quickly and appropriate roles had been tested and adopted. Thus the group had moved from a need for didactic inputs to a much less formal process of sharing, comparing and discussing common problems and experiences and the strategies which had now developed. The leader, however, continued to hold formal input sessions until one day the group removed all the impedimenta of teaching, for example, flip charts, markers, and so on, and left an empty chair in their discussion group. The point was taken and the role reassigned.

B1 Measurement of change

Definition and comment

It is difficult to assess the quantity and quality of change which occurs in a group or team over a period of time. It is even more difficult to be sure that noticed change has occurred directly as a result of what the group/team is doing, or even partially so, or whether it is a result of factors wholly extraneous to the group. The most important fact which has to be allowed for is that few of us, when starting a group or team, give much thought to preparing a detailed description of the point of departure. When it becomes desirable, necessary or even urgent, that we make some assessment of the progress of the group, there is little except highly subjective inaccurate memories of that point of starting. Change can only be measured if three factors are present: (a) there is a well-established baseline, (b) change can be defined and recognized, and (c) that there are instruments, no matter how crude, which can be used to measure that change.

Most instruments of measurement commonly used consist of some form of collective rating scheme in which subjective opinions about the quantity, direction and quality of change are made somewhat more objective by being collected from a number of people and compared. The common need of group-workers is to know whether a group is achieving its goals or whether something very different is occurring. Founded in this assessment may be so many very important things, for example, the continuation or termination of the group, a change of direction, contract, leadership, and so on, the continued support of the host organization, the members and significant others, the development of the recognition by leaders and members of the consequences of their in-group behaviour, the stage of the development of the group, and so on. Changes in feeling about a group or team which occur over time are but one of many possible themes of change, modification of behaviour, the generation of insight, acquiring skills, knowledge, understanding, mistakes, to be considered. The fact that measurement is directly linked to the onerous task of keeping some form of record is perhaps one of the main reasons why it is not a highly-developed groupwork skill.

Examples of problems

'How do I evaluate process and individual development within groups?'

'How do I assess the progress and the problems of a group?'

'How do I keep a comprehensive log of the group enabling me to know where it is?'

'How can I develop a more accurate, less subjective means of recording group and individual movement?'

'How can I monitor effectively, record and evaluate the groupwork in which I am involved?'

'In evaluation how can I find effective ways of discovering whether or not changes have occurred in individual group members?'

Analysis of problems

The problems stated here relate to the provision of some relatively objective form of measurement. In reality a very basic necessity because otherwise we are wholly in the shifting sands of the subjective response in any attempt, not only to justify the effective nature of the group approach, but more importantly to discover whether what we do within those approaches actually produces the results which we intend or indeed any result at all other than the comradeliness which can develop from being with similar people over a period of time. There is no really effective way of being wholly objective because for most group members their group constitutes only a small fraction of their existence, thus changes which occur within it may have their causation outside of it. Nevertheless, the fact that the group existed as a locus in which these changed behaviour patterns could be displayed is worthy of note in its own right. Basically, change of whatever nature can only be gauged against something which pre-existed it and which was reasonably well documented. The same factors which constituted this original documentation must then be reassessed in the same way at intervals and changes from previous states noted. What brought the noted changes about is a much more slippery customer, as is definition of their permanent or transient nature without a great deal of follow-up.

Useful ideas

Observation   On the basis of 'what you don't see you can't do anything about', I would rate the skill of observing group behaviour to be grossly undervalued and underexercised. Watching what group members do and what appears to happen as a result of what they do, which includes talking, is fundamental to even the most minimal degree of understanding of what the group is doing as opposed to what its most active member is about at any one time. Reactions to emitted behaviour are just as important as the precipitating behaviour itself, but they need to be seen – if they are not seen, through concentrating on an individual or even on one's inner thoughts, then they can't be known to exist. Then their constituent or causative role in generating some group behaviour at some later time will be ignored, which is one of the major factors underlying the common problem of attributing behaviour to entirely wrong causes. Bluntly it means that the evidence (or some of it) which would foster understanding, has been lost through lack of attention. Skill in observation does improve with practice but should not be confused with the ability to interpret what is seen, because the latter has many connotations with theoretical yardsticks. In any case many observations may remain remarkably unintelligible until later behavioural sequences offer additional evidence.

Attention

The time during which we can pay attention to anything as complex as group interaction, the quality of that attention, varies with an enormous number of factors ranging from interest, to the physical and psychological state that we are in during the group session. On top of this, as group and team leaders, there are other things to attend to including thinking about what is going on, analysing perceptions and making decisions, as well as playing whatever part in the group process which is ours to play. The experience of working with a co-leader, or taking part in observation exercises, is very rewarding as well as being somewhat frustrating, in that this can demonstrate how much attention it is possible to give when it is directed solely to one source, and also how much it is still easy to miss.

Content/process

I make no apology for including the ideas surrounding content and process here, for it is still remarkably obvious that the bias of attention is still heavily weighted in favour of content, that is, what is being said and the consequent neglect of process, that is, what is happening, takes place. So much has been written and talked about this, however, that I will content myself with one particular idea relating to this theme. Amongst the more basic reasons for using groups is that which is concerned with the location and use of the resources held in the group. In order to do this group members need to be sure that they have something to offer and that it is safe to offer it. This can only come about by learning from watching the responses received by others in the group. It is particularly important that the group or team leader should know these responses so that he/she can judge how to guide the group in its progress. Being exclusively interested in what group members are saying diminishes the likelihood of this understanding developing almost to the point of extinction.

Feedback

All organizations, large and small, show a high degree of correlation between efficiency and the extent to which they receive and *act upon* feedback on the consequences of their operation. This will obviously be considered in depth in the notes on strategies in this section.

Memory

Some consideration should be given to the basic ideas of recall, retention and selectivity, to immediate and long-term memory, to overlay, obliteration, and distortion, and in our particular business, to sequence, that is, ensuring as far as possible that events when recorded are in the actual sequence in which they originally occurred. Cause and effect are difficult enough to establish without the distortion of sequence. Of course, some form of recording is essential as so many things occur between one group session and the next, that sequences and intensities which span several sessions can never be recalled with sufficient accuracy without some reminder, preferably made soon after the events it charts.

Patterns

Group processes are in fact recurring patterns of behaviour which frequently escape attention due to our preference for responding to the smaller occurrences of which these patterns are constructed over longer periods of time. But it is beyond dispute that any understanding of the group, and the way it functions as entity or a unit as opposed to the individual behaviour of those who comprise it, can only arise from an overall grasp of these patterns. Just as it is equally true that any intervention which is directed at these patterns is powerfully effective at changing the life of the group as a whole.

Strategies

All forms of measurement require an estimation of the difference currently, or over time, between two or more points. Measurement in groupwork is the assessment of change between two points in time, A to B.

1 The establishment of a baseline

In effect this is establishing the nature of point A. It is not viable to say that the group or member has changed between points A to B if there is no record of the state that existed before the change process was started other than the subjective memory. So we use rating scales:

(a) Counting – the number of times a particular piece of behaviour which it is desired to change occurs within a given period.
(b) Rating – the intensity of emotional experience is evaluated upon a purely arbitrary scale again over a given period.

There are a large number of rating scales for a vast number of personal behaviours on the market, most of which employ a statistical analysis of the data obtained. In many instances they appear so complicated and so calculating that many groupworkers are frightened off or are scornful of their value. So be it. If you can establish at least some base at the beginning of the group, however crudely, AND RECORD IT, then subsequent assessments can be aligned to the base so established and some definite indication of movement noted.

This is not to say that any such movement which is noted can be clearly or definitely related to specific actions or experiences within the group. For instance, without complicated statistical analysis, it is not possible to rule out change which may have been brought about in the areas being measured by factors wholly outside the group. Thus the attribution of cause/effect is never totally precise but at least it is more accurate than subjective memory unless that has been particularly well trained.

2 Forms of measurement

(a) Application of those processes which established the base line at intervals of time to obtain the sequence of development.
(b) Self Report: (i) verbal, (ii) written. Verbal responses may be recorded as well but in both cases it is frequently necessary, at least, to suggest the lines of presentation. This is usually done by the presentation of questions to focus the responses (see, for instance, Garvin 1981: Chapter 8, one of the best presentations of methods of evaluating groupwork and of the instruments by which it is done; Preston-Shoot 1988. Other references are given at the end of this chapter).
(c) Feedback – again, either written or verbal is usually more effective when received by individuals from their fellow members collectively on the basis that those elements which are common to all comments are usually found to have substantial validity.

Carter (1954) put forward the thesis that in measuring the performance of individuals there are only three dimensions.

(i) Individual prominence – associated with aggressiveness, leadership, confidence and striving for individual recognition.
(ii) Group goal facilitation – for example, efficiency, adaptability, co-operation, and so on.

(iii) Group sociability – sociability, striving for group acceptance and adaptability.

3 Measurement of changes in the group

The instruments used may be exactly the same as for evaluating an individual member but they are applied to group performance, for example, the level of attainment of group objectives, the extent of the development, the level of cohesion, of attraction, the nature of the structure of the group and how well it is operating as a delivery system.

4 Measurement of changes in the containing environment

Once more the instruments are the same, but also included are the examination of opinions, written or verbal, offered by occupants of that environment and thus some interviewing may be necessary. There has to be some consideration of the ways in which the group may have affected its containing environment as well as the way that environment has affected the group.

5 External evaluation

This implies bringing someone who is not a member of the group into the situation to evaluate it. There are two principal ways in which this can be done:

(a) Direct observation – the assessor visits the group at intervals over its life time and records his/her observations, noting any significant changes.
(b) Tacit knowing – (a description coined by Polyani in 1968–9) in which the external assessor talks to the group members as individuals and from the totality of their comments creates a picture of what is happening in the group at selected points in its life.

It should not be beyond the bounds of individual groupworkers' ingenuity to devise his/her own methods and measures of measurement. There are just three fundamental points:

(a) It is necessary to know what changes, what areas of behaviour need to be measured, clearly and in specific terms.
(b) It is essential that right at the beginning markers should be laid down of the state of those change areas as a baseline.
(c) It is even more important that when ratings are made they should be recorded in some form which allows of comparison (for example, the elements must be the same) over time.

Example

A learning group was concerned with the quantity and quality of the take-up of information offered to them in lecture form. Knowing that there are many factors as, liking for the instructor, tiredness, illness, other preoccupations, and so on, which could affect the take-up of information, an instrument of assessment was designed. In essence this consisted of designing an input in which the actual number of bits of information was known and these were delivered without deviation from the script. Each member of the group was then able to count how many bits they had received and recorded. The differences were very interesting and included the recording of data which had not been part of the original input. But the overall average of the take-up encouraged the group members to devise methods of sharing records in all future direct informational input sessions, thus ensuring a much higher percentage cover of the available data. A later similar check recorded just such a large increase in the individual take-up.

Recall from one group session to another has several spin-offs. First, it tends to develop a better overall memory of events in each group member, but second, it also allows each member a second chance to integrate areas of previous experience which he/she had forgotten when the recall is done collectively and verbally.

DISCUSSION

This chapter has been concerned with those problems which arise from the group itself and is interesting in that some of those recorded problems were concerned not so much with assessment which has always had a large element of vagueness about it, as with concepts of comparative measurement. It must be clear that unless the practice of working with groups is to remain an exercise in 'flying by the seat of one's pants' then some clear correlation between effort, action, intervention, and so on, and outcome needs to be established both in general terms, but more importantly, the need of every groupworker to know more precisely what he or she is doing and why. Groups have a habit of swamping objectivity in the feelings that they commonly generate. Change can thus only be 'measured' on the basis of the establishment of some markers which are in more tangible form and less subject to biased recall than memory. Indeed it is only by the ongoing provision of such measurements that the elements of group design become something more than theoretical concepts.

Much of the material here is well covered in the textbooks, apart from the measurement aspect that is, and most of it is not very controversial, and I would recommend careful study of the literature, which, when ideas have been digested, can form the basis of a personal understanding to inform individual practice.

SECTIONAL REFERENCES

A1 Normative Structure

Diedrich, R. C. and Dye, H. A. (eds) (1972) *Group Procedures, Purposes, Processes and Outcomes*, Boston, Houghton Mifflin Co.

Douglas, T. (1979) *Group Processes in Social Work: A Theoretical Synthesis*, Chichester, John Wiley and Sons, 65–8.

Conformity, compliance, etc.

Allen, V. L. (1965) 'Situational factors in conformity', in L. Berkowitz (ed.) *Advances in Experimental Psychology*, vol. 2, London, Academic Press.

Aronson, E. (1976) *The Social Animal* (3rd edition), San Francisco, Freeman, Chapter 2.

Contract Negotiation

Bertcher, H. J. (1979) *Group Participation: Techniques for Leaders and Members*, London, Sage Publications, session 3.

Feldman, R. A. (1974) 'An experimental study of conformity behavior as a small group phenomenon', *Small Group Behavior* 5(4):404–26, London, Sage Publications.

Garvin, C. D. (1981) *Contemporary Groupwork*, Englewood Cliffs, NJ, Prentice-Hall.

A2 Subgroup structure

Dyads

Smith, D. (1978) 'Dyadic encounter: the foundation of dialogue and the group process', *Small Group Behavior* 9(2): 287–304, London, Sage Publications.

Subgroups ... almost any text on groupwork

Douglas, T. (1979) Ibid., 60–1, 189.

Golembiewski, R. T. and Blumberg, A. (1970) *Sensitivity Training and the Laboratory Approach*, Itasca, Illinois, F. E. Peacock Publishers.

Klein, A. F. (1972) *Effective Groupwork*, New York, Association Press.

A3 Open or closed group structure

Benson, J. F. (1987) *Working More Creatively with Groups*, London, Tavistock Publications, 29–30.

Douglas, T. (1979) Ibid., 88–9, 170.

Galinsky, M. and Schopler, J. H. (1987) 'Practitioners' views of assets and liabilities of open-ended groups', in J. Lassner, K. Powell and E. Finnagan (eds) *Social Groupwork: Competence and Values in Practice*, New York, The Haworth Press, Chapter 6.

Henry, M. (1988) 'Revisiting open groups', *Groupwork* 1(3): 215–28, London, Whiting and Birch.

Hill, W.F. and Gruner, L. (1973) 'A study of development in open and closed groups', *Small Group Behavior* 4(3): 355–61, London, Sage Publications.

A4 Role structure

Benne, K. D. and Sheats, P. (1964) 'The functional roles of group members', in J. W. Orton (ed.) *Readings in Groupwork, Selected Academic Readings*, Chapter 13.

B1 Measurement of change

Carter, L. F. (1954) 'Recording and evaluating the performance of individuals as members of small groups', *Personnel Psychology* 7:477–84.

Garvin, C. D. (1981) Ibid., Chapter 8.

Polyani, M. (1968–9) cited in Steinhauer, J. C. (1973–4) 'Tacit knowing as methodology for evaluating an encounter group', *Interpersonal Development* 4:1–20.

Preston-Shoot, M. (1988) 'A model for evaluating groupwork', *Groupwork* 1(2):147–57, London, Whiting and Birch.

Chapter 5

Problems relating to the conditions that affect the group

GENERAL AREA OF PROBLEM

No group exists in a vacuum. It is both part of a larger system and contains within itself smaller systems. Across its boundaries flows a traffic of influence in both directions. Thus a group influences, or can influence, the larger system in which it is embedded and most certainly that external system influences the performance and structure of the group.

One major problem in this area resides in the often unseen, unrecognized nature of these streams of influence which can lead to effects within the group being attributed to the more obvious visible possible causes, often with no other reason than that they are known about, while the real causes continue to operate in an unacknowledged but, nevertheless, powerful manner.

A group may be seen as an end point at which a collection of lines of influence and experience is gathered. Members of a group bring with them into the group all the baggage of their ongoing life outside of it – a lot of which must be unknown to the other members. Where the totality of the members' existence occurs in the context of the group, even then large parts of it remain hidden and internal, but the visible behaviour quotient is considerably extended.

The salient point is that whatever happens within the group as a unit/system is seldom, if ever, wholly and entirely sprung from causes within the group. Thus groupworkers are concerned that causation should be as visible as possible to lessen the hazards of wrongful attribution.

This chapter is therefore concerned with a constellation of problems related to the conditions in which a group has to function. Two major areas in this context are those conditions which are imposed by the properties of leaders and members, which, being covered by a separate section elsewhere in this text, will be omitted here. Those factors remaining divide into two main categories:

A Those conditions which may be termed external to the actual group.
B Those conditions which arise internally as a fact of the group's existence.

There is a complicating factor in this problem area and one which is very difficult to come to terms with, which is whether the constraints or condition has to be regarded for all realistic purposes as permanent, that is, unchangeable, or whether it has the potential, if appropriately dealt with, to change. The direction of that potential change also has complicating factors, bearing in mind that the major changes effected by intervention in social systems are seldom those which the change attempt was designed to bring about and are, as a consequence, usually unforeseen.

Under Category A the following subcategories have been presented:

A1 Organization and policy.
A2 Settings.
A3 Time.

Category B – the internal conditions – contains just two subcategories:

B1 The condition of size and number.
B2 Design.

PRESENTATION OF PROBLEMS CATEGORY A

A1 Organization and policy

Definition and comment

As already noted, the kind of groups we are interested in here bear the same relationship to larger systems as subgroups do to the groups in which they exist. Thus all groups are embedded in larger systems which often have the political, managerial and policy-making rights, only a small part of which is delegated to, or concerned with, the smaller system. Groups created, encouraged or allowed to occur within the ambit of such systems are thus influenced in many ways directly and indirectly, which has to be taken into consideration when designing a group and when assessing what it may be possible to achieve. Without question, large organizations create groups as part of policy without a very clear idea of whether what is being created can fulfil the functions allotted to it by reason of its position, the resources which it is given and even whether such a group is actually compatible with its parent system. This leads to considerable frustration for group and team leaders who may be as lacking in understanding of the true nature of the system in which they work as the managers of those systems are about the groups, units and teams they create in order to fulfil policy decisions, often made without any form of consultation.

Examples of the problems

'How can you deal with organizational pressure to regard people as counters for the games groupworkers want to play?'

'Colleagues' attitudes to groupwork and their lack of understanding of what is involved, leads to a great deal of difficulty.'

'Committee members and line managers as a general rule are not groupwork practitioners. They tend to feel that working in small groups is a poor use of resources. They permit groupwork but hedge it around with provisos, for example, minimum numbers, no cover for workers while they take groups, inadequate facilities and insufficient time, and so on, so that workers feel inhibited.'

'There is also the fear that groupworkers are fostering indiscipline amongst young people.'

'The support system is non-existent – I am expected to look to my line manager for support and I am reluctant to do so since the same individual is responsible for discipline.'

'I have the sense of being an outsider, of not really belonging to my team because of the demands of the organization.'

'How can I deal with the effects of the limits imposed by external power (finance) on the group's ability to act on group decisions?'

' "Groups" are being used in abundance by nursing staff with little regard to group formation or group dynamics because it is management policy.'

Analysis of problems

Blau and Scott (1980:101–15) defined organizations in terms of 'who benefits?'. The major problem is thus very logically how to achieve an equitable distribution of benefit for both those who are served by an organization and those who are members of it. It often appears to groupworkers and team members that organizations know little about teams and care less, and thus much energy is devoted to maintaining the organization in existence which, on the basic premise of a limited amount of energy being available, would automatically diminish that available for devoting to the work for which the organization exists.

Administrators are prone to point out an inalienable truth, which is that whatever it is that groupworkers and team members are engaged in, it represents but a small part of their overall concern. Thus the conditions under which administration actually expects groups and teams to function are seldom adequate, let alone ideal, largely because of an interplay of two main factors, namely, ignorance of the basic requirements for effective group functioning and even if understanding is present, pressure from conflicting demands for resources within the organization. Allocation of scarce resources is often controlled by factors other than need, for example, policy, publicity, interest, and so on, which leaves those at the working end of the organization with the distinct feeling that manipulative and somewhat cynical games are being played. This leads managers in turn to be resentful and to find reasons to denigrate, or at least diminish, what groupworkers and team members represent in value to the organization.

Perhaps one of the main points to be extracted from this state of affairs is a very simple one, which is that groupworkers and team members must develop a much greater understanding of the systems in which they work. Their expectations are so frequently based in the immediate prospect of the groups in which they work that they appear to regard frustration of those expectations as based in some kind of malicious intent on the part of management. Whereas what is often the case is that both partners see the system in which they operate from radically different viewpoints, and in particular the groupworkers have little or no ability to 'work' the system for the benefit of their clients or themselves.

Useful ideas

System thinking   Any group is a system, it exists in other systems and contains systems within it. In these circumstances it is remarkable how little attention is paid by groupworkers to this 'system of systems'. There is a strong tendency to create a group and to close the shutters on it in the mistaken belief that it can be isolated from its environment. It can't, and that environment will create influence effects on the group acknowledged by the group or not.

System playing   An idea which indicates that systems are there to be understood in terms of their operation and function and that this is an essential, though neglected, skill of any good groupworker, to know how to use that particular system in which his/her group is located, efficiently.

Interstices   In any system there are gaps. Some are known, some (many) are not. Often the creation of new units within an existing system goes through an elaborate process of integration only to find that the new units are very uncomfortably accommodated. Alternatively, the new units are created because they are required by some directive authority and are virtually left to fend for themselves (many Community Mental Handicap Teams were created in this way). But between the visible structures of the encapsulating system are many gaps which can often be occupied by some aspect of new units without detriment or massive cost, materially or financially, to the parent organization. These lacunae take the form of unknown but present resources and somewhat more frequently underused resources limited, not so much by their

	nature, as by the concept of their use maintained by the major system.
Communication	A common problem for groupworkers in a system is to rate their communication to others within that system on their own scheme of priorities, to phrase it in their own particular and often emotional language, to place it in the wrong form in the hands of the wrong people and without due consideration of the time schedule by which information is accepted into the system or by which decisions are made by it.
Consequence	The efficiency of a communication within a large system is related to the degree to which the consequences of ignoring it are perceived as more or less disastrous. In a world where multicommunications are competing for attention and possibly finance, this is a crucial factor.
Information	The quality of information and its presentation, the availability of information from other sources, all have to be considered.
Feedback	The system has not only a right but an essential need to know how a group or team is actually functioning unless stagnation is to become a way of life – but it must be given in ways which are relevant to the system as a whole.

There are many ideas relating to an enhanced understanding of the ways in which organizations are run and the ways in which policies are formulated or thrust into the system. Frequently the nature of information which would enable managers to make more effective policy decisions is not forthcoming or is not in usable form. I have found myself many times saying that the skill of the groupworker does not and should not be limited to the way he/she runs a group, but so little teaching about the nature of embedding and interdependency of systems has taken place that such a comment comes as a shock. We know that decision-making within a group can be wholly negated if that decision-making takes little or no cognizance of the constraints which the containing system can exercise. *Groups are never wholly independent of some constraining and containing system.*

Strategies

The primary strategy in this area starts from a realization of the embedded nature of all groups. Any group is part of some larger system or organization which can and does contain many other units and which also very probably has administrative and policy-making powers in a wide divergence of areas of interest. Thus this strategy is concerned with knowledge. It is essential for groupworkers to know about the system in which their groups are founded, at least the following basic facts:

(a) How is the system organized?

(b) Where does 'the group' or 'the team' fit into this system?

(c) Who or what position is responsible for immediate and also long-term decision-making which will directly or indirectly influence the process of the group or team?

(d) When and where are such decisions made?

(e) In what form should information from the group or team be presented in order to influence the decisions affecting them?

(f) What areas of autonomy exist for the group?

(g) If the 'normal' system does not or is not able to make essential decisions, to what other superior or external systems is it appropriate to make application?

It is essential that this kind of information should be available, especially to groupworkers operating within the ambit of large organizations, to counteract what is a most obvious system blindness. Ignoring the larger system is a recipe for disaster in that its influence is there shaping the outcomes whether acknowledged or not. Another factor in this strategy is the need of the group to generate information which can inform system decisions. It is a truism that any decision is only as good as the information upon which it is based. Groups which ignore the containing system are often ignored by it, especially when it comes to the allocation of resources and policy-making decisions. Much pressure which comes from management, for instance, on groups and teams, which is resented by their members because it seems not only irrelevant but also obstructive, is so because the decision to bring such pressure to bear is based upon an absolute scarcity of accurate information or understanding of what the group or team is attempting to do. Of course there are other reasons for such pressure including the need to secure results, or to divert resources as another area of the system becomes more visible, and so on.

Thus other strategies must be concerned with the nature of communication. Given that resource-allocation will be based upon either a directive from a higher authority or on some scale of current priority, the groupworkers and team-leaders have the need to be able to develop the skill of information presentation which will be effective in influencing decisions made under the latter heading.

The procedures under this strategy follow this kind of pattern:

(a) If possible discover the current order of priorities. If the group's activity is high on this list then very little problem exists – if on the other hand it is in the bottom half then a problem does exist.

(b) The nature of the group's presentation has to be such that it transfers the problem to the decision-makers in such a way that rejection is not inevitable.

(c) Decisions tend to be made between competing interests on the basis of the consequences for the system or organization that they entail:

(i)   thus all presentations for resources, or understanding must clearly indicate such connection between proposal and consequence. There is much pragmatic evidence to show that material which is presented in 'caring' or 'people' consequences terms, or even statistically, rates little attention, especially in competition where other material indicates clear and usually undesirable consequences as a result of being ignored;

(ii) the basic concept of groupwork, that behaviour is a more reliable indicator of a person than what they say, applies with equal force in this area too. A groupworker or team-leader who is able to translate the aims, objectives, achievements and needs of his/her group or team into terms which are relevant to managerial thinking, is in a strong position to achieve the group or team ends.

This is not sophistry or connivance. Consider how much groupworkers strive to modify and adapt the forms of thinking of group members by introducing them to a different perception of situations and of behaviour and of social inter-actions. This is merely the same educating process applied in a different direction and a basic understanding of the fact that all explanation has to be presented to and tied into previous knowledge.

Videos of groups have sometimes been used to convey directly what is happening. The inconvenience of this is the time which is taken in the process and the fact that few videos can escape the stultifying effect of the recorder limitation, for example, how many group members are visible at any one time?

A2 Settings

Definition and comment

It is remarkable how the environment in which a group is held has such influence on the way in which that group performs. To a great extent the setting dictates a large amount of the aims and objectives of the group and both directly and indirectly constrains the manner in which those aims can be achieved. For our purpose then, a setting is defined as the immediate context in which the group performs. It possesses an ethos, aims and objectives, rules and constraints of time, a tradition or traditions and exercises power and influence in various ways, defined and obscure. Any group therefore, set up within the ambit of a setting, is part of an organizational structure which is attempting to achieve, sustain, support or maintain a given programme. Thus the efficacy of a group will be judged not so much on its functioning *qua* group, but on the degree to which it contributes to that given programme. A large number of problems in this area arise from this fact, that is, that groupworkers create successful groups in the sense that they function as groups effectively and obviously serve to meet the needs of their members, but they are not seen by the containing organization as contributing to the overall programmes. Conversely, organizations often have expectations of groups which are wholly unrealistic given the setting in which they are obliged to function.

Examples of problems

'Induction groups are considered a good approach in probation but the problem of voluntary or compulsory attendance and the prospect of clients being "breached" creates group members who attend but contribute nothing.'

'How is it possible to integrate groupwork into the unit setting – we are dealing with assessment and rehabilitation of the elderly.'

'How can a group take responsibility for itself and its decisions in a setting where the power of the group is strictly limited?'

'In a setting which traditionally works on a one-to-one basis, my colleagues demonstrate a lack of understanding of what is involved and frequently situations arise which are detrimental to groupwork.'

'I have been involved with Intermediate Treatment activity groups for several years. They have seemed always to be all activity and very little about shared group experience.'

'It is very difficult when running a group in a school room to counter the effect of the room and its reminder of school days.'

'In a residential setting the role conflict is difficult to deal with. Staff are expected to be authoritative in their ordinary roles and this carries over into the social and life-skill groups and makes a barrier.'

Analysis of problems

It is good that groupworkers have begun to realize that the actual physical setting in which a group operates can have a considerable and sometimes inimical effect upon the participants. In the main groupworkers make allowances for the expectation that group members may have about the group and are aware that rumours and lack of real understanding influence the way members will present and will condition what they hope to get out of the experience. But less attention seems to be paid to the expectations generated by a physical environment which may have very strong connotations of pleasure or pain or indifference in their past experience.

Second, the actual ethos of an organization under whose aegis a group operates may also create hampering expectations. An element of punishment which is seen to reside in some probation work has been known to be responsible for a reduction in commitment to a group to the mere presentation of bodies at the appropriate time and place.

Third, there is evidence that the relationship of groupwork, or at least of a particular kind of groupwork, to the function of a pre-existing system has not been thought through. Groupwork like this is part of the 'good idea' syndrome and the way such a subsystem has to integrate with the larger system in which it will operate receives little attention. Much potential conflict, frustration and distress is built into the situation in this way. In any setting a group or team has to be a way of furthering, developing, complementing or adding to the system function already in existence. Even if such a group or team is created in order to bring about change in the host system it still needs the basis of a genuine understanding of that system and of the relationship between part and whole, to work from.

Useful ideas

Ethos

This is defined as the 'characteristic spirit and belief of a community, person or literary work' (*Oxford Paperback Dictionary*, 1979). What is important about it is that the 'characteristic spirit' is often tangible enough and powerful enough to be a major influence on the way that groups held within its ambit actually perform. One of the problems related to this is that of unfamiliarity, that is, people who work within an organization and are immersed in its ethos become so accustomed to it that they cannot appreciate the effect that it may have on those not so familiar.

Environmental constraints

Most groups/teams exist in organizational systems which have been created to achieve sometimes very complex and sometimes essentially simple ends. During the time of their existence they have created boundaries within which actions will be either tolerated or accepted as ways of doing things. Often the concepts of groupwork lay somewhat across these ideas which then appear to act as constraints despite the fact that the groupwork may ultimately be more than justified as a method of achieving just those goals which the organization holds dear.

Expectation

Settings are special environments which are ideally those which facilitate the performance of the task which the system, which engendered them, had in mind. But their existence over time generates traditions and expectations in terms of the essential focus of work and the ways of doing the work. Interest may be diffuse, time may be limited and set by a situation over which the settings-system has little or no control. It is wise to discover before establishing a group or team how firm and important these expectations may be and if they have to be accepted, how that will influence the design of the group/team and what it can achieve.

Strategies

Much of what was said under the previous section is applicable here. The only real difference is one of scale. The organization is large and the setting in which a group exists is small or at least smaller. There are three factors to take into consideration:

1 Potential group members will have expectations of any setting in which a group is held which will relate to their experience, direct or indirect, of such a setting.
2 The actual material situation can influence the way a group functions within it and not just in terms of immediate physical comfort but also in more esoteric ways like colour, light, and atmosphere.
3 Settings already have basic aims before groups are established within them and especially if the groups are seen as extending, changing or moving outside these aims, or even the ways in which they are normally achieved, some constraint may be placed upon them.

There is a very strong need in all settings to seek at least understanding if not direct approval of how a proposed group will contribute to the aims and purposes of the setting in which it is established. Of course some groups, while being part of the activity of one organization, are held in the setting of another and unrelated system because of considerations of space, and so on. The factors of expectation and of material situation are still strongly applicable, but the aims of the host organization probably less so.

Example

A probation officer established a group for several of his male adolescent clients because he had discovered that they all came from similar family backgrounds and part of their problem was the kind of response they produced, and the attitudes they held, towards adult discipline. The group was established in the probation office of a small country town and the sessions were chaotic. These lads could not be induced to talk about their attitudes to discipline and adult authority. Their verbal ability was low and their action quotient consequently very high. In desperation the group leader arranged for them to spend a long weekend at an isolated cottage being turned by the department into a field centre, where they were engaged in the heavy manual labour of road building across the moorland. From incidents which occurred during this work the problems of discipline, authority and adult power became manifest and the subject of intense and often heated discussion. The immediacy of behaviour and discussion acted as a 'reality' trigger and eventually comparisons between the immediate experience and the attitudes and behaviour which had got them into trouble in the first instance were brought out and studied.

In this case the strategy had been to use a setting which was not only action-intensive but also much closer to work and everyday activity than the probation office and talking in cold blood about something about which the lads had little or no ability to verbalize.

A3 Time

Definition and comment

Time is one of the most fascinating of factors in groupwork. In most cases groupworkers appear to have little true understanding of how long it takes for events to occur. Thus constant questions are asked as 'How many sessions should my group take?, 'How long should each session be?, 'What kind of period elapses before the group moves into the next stage of development?', and so on. Guidelines about how long this or that should take are at best very rough rules of thumb, but in general most events take far longer to occur than even experienced groupworkers expect. Which is only really what would be expected. Consider how many major components of a group are of different quality to those in another group. The leader – personality and skill, aims and constraints; the members – qualities, experience, abilities, expectations, inter-actions, and so on. What is always astounding is that similar patterns emerge in all groups. The constituents of the patterns are different in quality and intensity but never in kind, and the time intervals between recognizable stages of pattern-growth may be widely different in different groups, but if the group lasts long enough those recognizable patterns do develop. Of course, where time is arbitrarily limited then group design has to take this fact fully into account in one of two ways, either by restricting aims and methods to what is knowntobe achievable within the set limit, or to attempt to achieve more by substitution, for example, by increasing intensity of interaction within the allotted time.

Examples of problems

'I do not have adequate time to devote to the groupwork task. I need time to get to know the people I work with as people – not just use them as cogs in my machine.'

'I seem to manage the time badly.'

'I didn't have time to deal with emergencies – because I am a part-timer, they do not always happen in my office time.'

'Picking up the group dynamic from one group session to the next always after a fortnight's break and frequently with small changes in attendance, is very hard.'

'I can be unrealistic about what can be achieved in limited time. All my groups have to be run on top of my usual case load – having sufficient time to plan, assess the group and develop group leaders was a major problem especially as one of the leaders was a volunteer in full-time employment.'

Analysis of problems

I think the major problem in this category relates specifically to a lack of data. Groupworkers establish groups using purely arbitrary time boundaries which they have arrived at from general trends relating to particular kinds of groups. But material which would indicate a more elaborate assessment of the time required to achieve particular group outcomes is virtually unknown. Because of the 'unique' nature of each group many believe that the time needed to establish its goals can only arise out of a process of discovery within the group itself and that similar previous groups were so individual as to be a wholly unreliable guide to current needs. This is not so. Human behaviour tends to conform to patterns which, allowing for the idiosyncratic nature of the elements within a group (a system which incidentally tends to restrict the number of presentations of these patterns quite markedly), can be shown to operate within normal time spans.

Until groupworkers can present to the organizations in which they work pragmatic evidence of the time-scales of what they are being asked to do, their management will, in the absence of relevant data to the contrary, have expectations that are restricting, frustrating and probably counter-productive. As we shall see later, the sovereign remedy for this problem resides in the collection of appropriate data and of its relevant but simple analysis. Many groups succeed and some fail, but whereas in the second instance there is often a kind of post-mortem, the former is accepted as something that was inherent in the group-work process. Different workers proceed at different speeds, groups in the same system have different component individuals whose individuality affects the time intervals at which development sequences are achieved. It should not be, nor is it, beyond the wit of workers to achieve some rudimentary scaling of progress which takes account of the known effects of difference and makes a reasonable estimate of the consequences of that which may originally have been unforeseen. If this were to happen we should find many more groupworkers saying 'It is not possible in that form and within that time' and less lamenting of the fact that they were apparently prevented from achieving what they assumed to be possible by poor time management, inappropriate group design and wholly inappropriate allocations of time.

Useful ideas

Scale and proportion   After workshop sessions with groupworkers I am nearly always left with some surprise at the time-scales which they work to. When we think how long people have taken to acquire their behavioural patterns in their current form, how quickly do we expect that they can be changed, redirected or modified in some way? What proportion of a person's total daily existence is spent in a group? It is possible that intensity of experience can be brought into play to balance the small amount of time a group experience endures for the individual member. But unless accelerating gambits are used, even to develop intensity requires time if only to prepare adequately the support system in which it will be appropriate. In any case most group members will have different rates at which they can absorb and integrate the experience the group is offering. There are very definite costs to be defrayed for attempting to move a group faster than some of its members are prepared to go – likewise there are costs in restraining those willing and eager to move on. They have to be considered in the overall needs of the group.

Behavioural exposure

Groupworkers frequently talk about the development of 'trust', that is, trust which is relevant to certain kinds of ingroup behaviour. Analysis of the development of trust in groups shows it is related directly to a personal sense of safety within the group which in turn appears to be related to group members having witnessed behaviour patterns similar to those they wish to emulate, and having noted not once, but several times, the responses that these patterns have elicited, and have developed as a result a sense of optimism of the successful outcome of their own venture. But whereas rules can be expressed verbally in a short space of time, it can take considerably longer for members to satisfy themselves by direct observation of the consequences of certain patterns of behaviour.

Holding

This concept relates to those techniques used by group leaders to hold group members in the group while the basic behavioural exposure takes place and the beginning levels of trust are allowed to develop. Often the time involved is undercalculated and allowances are not sufficiently made for the suspicion which some group members may have for the group in the first place, for whatever reason that may be.

Developmental patterns   This is one of the most documented ideas in group-work and so will only be mentioned briefly here. Fundamentally it states that groups evolve through stages of a life cycle; that these stages are not necessarily linear; that they can be recognized; that the group's potential to work changes, often significantly, from one stage to another; that there is the possibility of regressive and reiterative stages; that the sequence is markedly different for open and for closed groups, and finally that there are rough estimates of the time that given kinds of groups may take to traverse at least some of these stages. There are also between session patterns, and cyclic patterns, which can only be really recognized for what they are through the process of recording and of scanning those recordings.

Time management   The basis of time management in working with groups and teams is quite simple, it involves having a reasonable idea of the time that the major group operations require and incorporating that into the original group design. Thus when a request for a group to be employed is received its possibility in the form suggested can be assessed in terms of the time required:

1 The time the groupworker has available.
2 The duration of each group session.
3 The number of sessions required.

Strategies

First, it is necessary to find out how long it takes, or conversely, if there is only a given amount of time, what can be achieved:

1 There are several branches to the primary strategy here:

   Check the literature very carefully and note the correlation between various aspects of time, aims and outcomes. Quite a large number of times for groups are set almost arbitrarily and in some recorded instances this is clearly stated as having a major effect on outcomes. Also recognize that there are four principal time aspects:

   (i) Sessional duration – the time spent continuously on one session in a series.
   (ii) Spacing – the time between one session and the next.

    (iii)   The life time – which is usually only applicable to closed groups which have a definite life.

    (iv)   Contact time – which is the time an individual member spends in contact with the group.

This process should help a groupworker to begin to establish certain rough data, for example, how long it takes for the actual development of the group as a unit indicated by a commitment to the group in different kinds of problem/member situation. (Some authorities maintain that the minimum time for achieving this situation, even in conducive circumstances, is about twelve contact hours with a *closed* group.) General data from the literature make a good starting point which can often be supplemented by the addition of material from discussion with other groupworkers.

The knowledge which arises in this way most often indicates two rather surprising facts. First, that the generation of a *working group* starting from scratch tends to take much longer than the expectations of such a time that are generally held and a great deal longer if the group is dealing with members who could be classed amongst those who are extremely suspicious of all kinds of approaches. Second, that extremely short, that is, one-off sessions, can produce satisfactory outcomes in certain circumstances. Usually those circumstances are either an immediate response to a critical situation or, more usually, they are a very carefully designed approach to a group already in existence with the intent of coping with one very clearly defined aspect of their situation.

With regard to spacing, there is some evidence that given a similar quality of leadership, groups in a single session of six hours and groups having six one-hour sessions spaced over several weeks, show little difference in outcome, but considerable difference in their levels of cohesion and some difference in their ability to relate what they are doing in the groups to life outside them (Susan El-Shamy 1978).

2 Recording

My insistence on the value of recording is based upon much experience of working with groupworkers who are having problems but who have so little valid data about what has been happening in their groups that to establish cause and effect connections is well-nigh impossible. Methods of recording need only to be simple but they should be (a) sequential, (b) written or recorded, (c) formed from as many sources as can be made available, (d) made in such a way that it is comparatively easy to scan them in sequence to ascertain the larger developmental patterns of the group thus:

(i)   Try to have visual access to a clock and mentally register the main group events. Develop a sequential recall system by practising recall preferably checked against some objective recording or the recall of another member or co-leader.

(ii) Record as soon as possible after the group session including the time-markers noted. Audio recordings may be valuable in the early days of recording mastery, but they are time consuming both to make, to listen to, and almost impossible to cross-refer or scan for a long-term sequence.

(iii) Use the group to recall what occurred in the session; not only does this serve to bring to light material which would be otherwise overlooked, it creates involvement and also helps the development of a greater clarity of understanding about how the group is functioning.

Only from recorded material of this nature can the individual groupworker begin to assess the accuracy of the time values which have been built into the group design.

A simple record sheet should be designed which compels a form of systematic recording:

TIME	OBSERVATION		COMMENT
	CONTENT	PROCESS	

I have found that, depending on the sessional duration of the group, the time column is best divided into equal time bites of about ten or fifteen minutes. This quickly becomes a well-established habit which then does not need constant reference to clock or watch during the group sessions (which action has the probability of being both irritating to group members and capable of misinterpretation). Because of our obvious interest in what people are saying it is advisable to limit entries in the content column and concentrate more on what effect what is being said has on the group, which should then be recorded in the process column.

I find that when reading records later certain correlations at greater or lesser distance in time tend to emerge. These connections can then be recorded in the comments column and lines and arrows link related factors.

3 Time constraint

In many groups the major time elements are often set by considerations other than those which would best serve the group's interests. A damage-limitation exercise then becomes necessary:

(a) What time elements would ideally be set to achieve the aims of the proposed group? Cover all four time aspects.
(b) What are the time elements dictated by the circumstances in which it is proposed to operate?
(c) Are any of these dictated times subject to a possible revision to a more favourable state?
(d) State the discrepancy between the two sets of time elements including probable revisions.
(e) What elements of the original group aims is it now possible to achieve in the time structure available, bearing in mind that it is better to redesign extensively and ensure success than to enter into what may well be a 'no-win' situation and the damage this could entail?

A major element of redesign in constrained time circumstances lies in the reduction of very general aims to much more specific ones. Another is to increase the intensity of contact as a compensation for loss of time, which may involve using a closed group in preference to an open group and also in reducing the numbers involved. A third area of compromise may lie in changes of leadership styles. Time-limited groups with a clear and defined task can be very effective with a directive leader.

If the purpose of the group entails a natural growth situation where group numbers need 'to be held' until they have seen enough to be experienced within it to be reasonably certain what to expect, then the time element needs to take into consideration the rate at which an appropriate level of such experience can be achieved. There are exercises which have the effect, when successful, of accelerating this process, but considerable evidence points to the fact that trust developed in this way has a somewhat unsubstantial and insecure base. It is preferable, where circumstances allow, to use gentle encouragement to stimulate progress and to be particularly ready to take advantage of those situations which occur naturally within the ambit of the group's normal business. Development established in this way tends to be much better integrated by the group members and does not have large elements of the 'public conformity' syndrome about it.

PRESENTATION OF PROBLEMS CATEGORY B

B1 Size and number

Definition and comment

The size of a group is in fact defined by the number of participating members it has. Number, because it is so obvious, has been a favourite experimental variable for many years and researchers have filled the pages of many books and articles with the effects different levels of membership can have. Indeed, one of the first questions that is likely to be asked by a group of aspiring group-

workers relates to the appropriate size of a group. To which the logical answers
– it depends upon how many people are available or suitable, how many you
can handle, what kind of group is being set up for what purpose, how much
time is available and so on and so on – are not seen as being all that helpful.
Nevertheless, they go some way to establishing a crucial factor of group life,
which is that all the variables are interdependent; that in essence a good group
is one that combines the essential variables in proportions which are most
suitable for the job it has been set up to perform. The corollary of this is also of
paramount importance, which is that when a reasonable and harmonious
balance cannot be achieved because one or more of the essential variables is
fixed in an inappropriate way, then this has to be accepted as influencing the
whole combination and ultimately the probable outcomes. Such inappro-
priately-fixed variables may sometimes be counterbalanced by substitution or
differential employment of others, but this has to be a consciously designed and
off-setting process and is dependent on a clear understanding of the possible
consequences of design factors like size.

Examples of problems

'I really don't know how size affects group performance.'

'The selection of numbers is out of my hands – there is a lack of choice –
members are drafted.'

'The balance of different kinds of members – how many of one or another –
is hard to judge.'

'Members fluctuate because different clients come on different weeks
making continuity a problem.'

Analysis of problems

I think the problem quoted first above probably expresses the crux of the
situation, that is, groupworkers have not really clarified the relationship of
group size to the possible consequences. Judging by the comments I have
received, a concept of appropriate group size bears a striking similarity to
the first, or most impressive statement, verbal or written, which indicated
a preferred number seen or heard by the beginning groupworker. What was
not taken into account often enough was that this preferred number was what
one worker, with one particular kind of group with particular aims in a special
setting, had discovered maximized group achievement. As most of the early
literature on groups was psychotherapeutic in origin in this country, the
numbers found appropriate for their groups seem to have created an indelible
impression, despite the fact that for most other kinds of workers such size
and such approaches are mainly inappropriate for the work they are trying to do.

Second, as stated earlier, the size of a group may be determined by factors other than those of rational choice by the group convenor. Where this occurs, as when any major group-design element is fixed arbitrarily by circumstances, then the original intentions should be modified in order to take cognizance of the probable consequences of this inflexibility.

Useful ideas

Like group development this is a much-written-about area of groupwork. I can be sure when meeting beginning groupworkers that they will have got some ideas of the best size for a group, usually it is a purely arbitrary figure culled from the literature, and the basic concept of a size as a design element which can be varied to enhance or diminish aspects of the group's performance, has yet to be learnt. The ideas stated here are well-covered elsewhere and are introduced here as a brief reminder. (For a more detailed run down on group size see Hare (1962: Chapter 8) and for a chart of the comparative effects see Douglas (1979:88).)

Visibility	Small groups ensure a high level of visibility, of exposure of all their members.
Hiding	Conversely, large groups have reduced levels of overall exposure of members and allow of the possibility of hiding (sometimes necessary).
Relationships	*Intensity* – small groups tend to foster stronger and more intense relationships.
	Numbers – large groups have the potential of developing a greater number of interpersonal relationships.
Ideas	Large groups potentially have more ideas, more resources available, though access to them may be more difficult.
Guidance	Smaller groups have a lesser need for guidance and leadership – but weaker perception of the competence and ability of the group.
Attitudes	Smaller groups tend to show less change in the attitudes and responses of members – in other words, smaller groups tend to confirm their members.
Relationship to task	When constraints allow, the size of a group should bear a direct relationship to the task it is to perform, bearing in mind the known effects of size.

Strategies

1 Read what has been written in the literature about size, being very careful to

distinguish what kind of groups, created under what kind of circumstances, the data are derived from.

2 Learn to apply the known correlations between group size and effect. Hare (1962) lists five such points of correlation:

(i)   Size and satisfaction.
(ii) Size and the emergence of leadership.
(iii) Size and the increasing number of relationships.
(iv) Size and the time for communication.
(v)   Increased resources and diminishing returns.

These five points should be considered in the following terms:

(a) Thus in general a group in which one of the primary aims is to develop close and intimate relationships should be small in number, the larger the group the greater the possible level of individual dissatisfaction.

(b) Where it is required as part of the group process that the leader(s) (and other members) need to be keenly observant of each other and thus of the consequences of behaviour in the group, this is a task which is more effectively performed in smaller groups. There is an estimated limit of seven to eight people that any one person can observe and be involved with in the context of a group depending of course upon the kind of activity.

(c) Hare offers $$x = \frac{3^n - 2^{n+1} + 1}{2}$$

where x = the number of potential relationships
n = the number of individuals.

This formula produces increases in potential relationships as follows:

size of group	number of relationships
2	1
3	6
4	25
5	90
6	301
7	966

These figures include the potential relationships between subgroups as well as the relationships between individuals. Of course nowhere near the larger number of relationships will develop in any one group, but it must be borne in mind that a large potential relationship factor mitigates against the development of intimate relationships. It is also interesting to note that in larger groups if the leadership is directive in the sense of restricting communication patterns for all members to one of direct interaction with the leader, then this pairing situation reduces the number of potential relationships and can be a strategy used to avoid decreasing group numbers. There are other group consequences as well.

(d) Given that a group session occupies a stated period of time, then the time available pro rata for each member openly to communicate within such a group decreases with increased numbers. Thus, strategically, the higher the degree of individual communication that is required the smaller the group should become. It is also noticeable that as groups increase in size distribution of participation skews so that a few members begin to occupy much more of the group's time and some occupy a great deal less. Thus where communication problems are an essential reason for a group's existence, it is wise to recognize that size is a very important facilitating or restricting factor.

(e) Increases in size imply an increase also in the resources available to the group, but there is a point, varying depending upon the essential task of the group, when an increase in numbers produces a diminishing return in terms of resources. There are several possible reasons for this:

(i)   Access – increasing numbers beyond a point may create difficulties in co-ordinating and in getting across to the resources theoretically available.

(ii) Threat – large numbers may decrease the input to the group by members who feel inhibited by the possibility of exposure to a greater number of people.

(iii) Optimum size – some tasks require a given number of people for maximum achievement, the addition of others reduces the competence of the group through the matter of interference.

(iv) Consensus – more ideas may be available from larger sizes of group but there is also the probability that consensus will be much harder to achieve.

For all these reasons the essential strategy with regard to group size comprises two major responses:

1 The selected size should be compatible with the major aims of the group and thus facilitative, or

2 If numbers are not controllable (for example, in a family group), then due consideration should be given to the consequences of this constraint.

Much of this emphasis will be reasserted in the following section on the design of groups.

B2 Design

Definition and comment

To refer to what is more usually called planning or preparation as 'design' is deliberate. It stresses that using the basic elements which are common to all groups, any single group should be set up using that combination of those basic elements which is possible to meet the needs of those who will be its members or its sponsors or both in the light of the best knowledge available at the time. This puts the emphasis squarely on the groupworker to have substantial knowledge in three areas: (1) of the basic elements of group construction, (2) of the ways in which they may be combined to work towards given ends, and (3) of the needs which it is proposed to meet by the construction of any particular combination. This runs counter to the idea that a groupworker masters a limited range of combinations of basic elements, selected on the basis of a particular theoretical creed, whereby group participants tend to be fed into roughly the same system almost irrespective of the fact that their real needs could have been more effectively met by another group form.

As some of the examples make abundantly clear, the knowledge of how group elements can be combined to meet given situations is not readily available and even when known, the knowledge of the situation upon which the combination was based is frequently inadequate. There is also the fact that being a member of a group brings about changes in need and in priorities so that few designs are not subject to redesign as basic components change in value.

There is ample circumstantial evidence that time spent in the design stage of a group pays enormous dividends in many ways – not least that as far as possible elements which are inhibitive of a group's success are not built into it, are avoided altogether, or the design is structured to allow as far as possible for their unavoidable presence. There is also the learning process which occurs when designs are seen to work or not work, when analysis can reveal why. Too many groupworkers are, in my opinion, so satisfied when their groups go well that they neglect to ask why.

Examples of problems

Many examples in this area took the form of 'How do I plan my group?'

'Some people think you can set it up and it just happens – there's a sort of myth about a group's natural dynamism.'

'What part of the lives of potential members needs focusing on in the group?'

'There are problems, for example, inadequate information, in identifying member need.'

'When should you plan to use an open group?'

'I believe planning is two-thirds of good groupwork, but thoughts rarely become reality.'

'I would like to have the skill which learns from past failures in running future successful groups.'

'Planning groups in advance is still very important for me although I might end up having to reassess the direction I may be taking within the group when it actually takes place.'

Analysis of problems

Much, which would have been relevant here, has already been said in a comment section. But several points may be stated briefly:

1 Design or planning for a group when well done serves to eliminate having to do excessive repair work during the course of the group.
2 It throws into bright relief the kind of information and of understanding which is necessary for planning to be really effective.
3 It also highlights the essential interdependence of the elements of design.
4 Because a design is only as good as the information and knowledge available at the time of its creation there evolves the strong need to develop a method of reassessment and consequent redesign as information and knowledge are changed by experience.

The quotation above about having 'the skill to learn from the past' is extremely relevant. I have been made aware over the years how much group-workers seem to enter into a new group situation either almost as if they had never been in a group before, or as if all groups were absolutely in all respects the same, rather than that they all possess similar patterns. In either case the adaptation of basic design elements is ignored in favour of absolute uniqueness or of an absolute similarity.

Useful ideas

Interdependence	All design elements are wholly enmeshed at all kinds of different levels. In an existing group it is scarcely possible to change one design element, for example, size, without generating change either of kind or of quality in all the other elements.
Appropriateness	The combination of design elements needs to be chosen in the light of existing knowledge for the expressed needs of its members and of the organization which has fostered it. The actual progress of a group will often reveal inadequacies of its design and it is wholly appropriate that a renegotiated design should occur.
Level of knowledge	A knowledge of design elements and the extent to which they are required is a major groupwork asset. This knowledge is required primarily for the effective design of groups, but also to generate awareness of, in those situations where the factor of choice over the kind and

quality of certain design factors is beyond the immediate control of the groupworker, the effect such constraints will have and whether a group is at all possible.

Preparation   This is basically a form of design but it is concerned less with the design elements of a group than with assuring that one has done all things which might ensure a reasonable launch for the group (see, for instance, Hodge 1977).

Strategies

1 Information

Any preparation for a group needs two basic elements of information:

(i)   for the designer to know what the design elements are;
(ii) to have an assessment of what combination of them at what level of intensity would best meet the needs of the proposed group members.

Neither of these elements can be known with great precision but that is no excuse for not obtaining information to whatever level can be made available. A good working list of the factors which play some part in constraining a group and must therefore be given due consideration in planning (the strength and effect of these constraints will vary from situation to situation), is to be found in Douglas (1979:184–5).

Example

The design of groups within a prison included a timetable of attendance which was well suited to the needs of the prisoners involved and was very carefully constructed to avoid clashing with any other major activity. Yet consistently group members did not attend because they were otherwise engaged by other staff members. The essential design element which had been overlooked was the need to obtain the understanding co-operation of other members of staff to what was, for this institution at that time, a new venture.

2 Analysis

By far one of the most helpful strategies in the design of groups for specific purposes is to look very carefully at past experiences in similar situations. This is not possible, of course, unless a reasonable degree of recording exists. It is axiomatic that when a group goes wrong groupworkers hold a post-mortem in order to discover the possible causes. But in my experience few bother to analyse the group that went right. In one sense each group is a new adventure but in another it is an opportunity to apply what has been learnt from previous groups. The successful group is not just a matter for congratulations but a real opportunity to answer the question 'Why?'. It may be disheartening to discover how much of the success was due to factors over which the groupworker had little or no control. But it is essential, if one is to be less dependent upon chance factors, and to begin to know what works and why, that such an analysis should be made.

Example

An experienced groupworker had carefully examined his groups over a period of years and realized that his strong point was the ability to create a structure within which his clients worked well and with considerable success. When he started work with a different client group he began to realize that he was not as successful as he was accustomed to be in developing a group which worked. When he scanned his recording of the group what emerged fairly clearly was that the design for the group had not given sufficient weighting to the emotional needs of his new clients. In his next group the worker enlisted the help of a colleague as co-worker who was noted for her sensitivity to the emotional needs of group members.

3 Consequence

It is also essential to know the consequences of varying the design elements one against another and to know the degree of intensity any element needs in order to produce certain consequences. One of the main elements of design is time and this has been discussed earlier in this chapter. But it is often obvious that groupworkers have no clear perception of how much time, at what intensity of interaction, is necessary to achieve a given result. Thus they set out to change entrenched attitudes in groups whose overall time span can be measured in hours, little realizing that much longer periods would be appropriate.

Pragmatic information from those who have tried is worth gold. The isolation in which a lot of groupworkers operate, often self-imposed, means that they are constantly having to reinvent the wheel. We hold one of the basic truths about the effectiveness of groupwork to be that it induces members to share, but we seem very reluctant or incapable of including our colleagues in this process.

The ultimate point about group design is that although we emphasize the setting-up processes in this respect, the quality of information available in this stage is such that inevitably more and different information will become available during the course of a group's life, unless it be extraordinarily short. Thus major design factors may be set at the beginning but the design must also allow for constant agreed modification to the design parameters to take place when the need becomes evident. It must also be obvious that a group which has been in existence for several sessions is, in most essentials, the same as when it started, but because some form of change is probably an important reason for its existence, many factors may well show some change, attitudes will have modified, needs for defence and security will probably have reduced, the realization of potential, and so on, will have developed. A certain amount of adjustment to the system in consideration of these changes is necessary. Design is thus not a one-off exercise but a constant exercise to maintain the most productive and effective delivery system that is possible.

DISCUSSION

For generations groupwork text books have had pertinent things to say about group size. I have a sneaking suspicion that this occurred not because there was a considerable amount of valuable information available about the effects of different sizes of groups, but that size is an extremely visible factor. So the quality of information about size and its practical effects still makes it inevitable that a groupworker in the last decade of the twentieth century can say 'I really don't know how size affects group performance'.

If, as I believe, the basic, bottom-line skill of group leadership resides in the ability to see what is happening, then the kinds of question to which tyro groupworkers need to have answers are as follows:

How many people is it possible to observe in a group?
What variations are there under special circumstances, that is,
– heavy personal involvement,
– dispersive activity,
– particular kinds of group goals?
How is it possible to combine the observations of several leaders?

Because of the many-role position of a group leader, the anxieties in that situation are added to by the realization that concentration on member-behaviour and consequence becomes so thinly spread that to all intent it has lost some individual members from its scan.

In a simple and direct way this highlights what is a common problem of all the sections in this group, which is that because so much emphasis has always been placed on the operational skill of running a group, on the warmth engendered and on the power involved, in the pleasure of working with individuals and in being able to be helpful, enabling, facilitating, curative, therapeutic and supportive, so little has been devoted to the structure, or to employ an overused modern term, the infrastructure, which defines, creates, supports, maintains and almost ensures the success of the group.

Until a few years ago groupwork stressed planning to some extent but ignored the embedded nature of groups and the cross-boundary seepage of influence. There was very little available information on the linked and inter-dependent nature of the processes which were being isolated in academic research. But the plain fact remains and stubbornly makes its presence felt in all group activity that to change any structural or functional element in a group produces a concomitant change, great or small, positive or negative, in every other factor as well.

Thus heavy stress has to be placed upon the groupworker's need to develop and use those skills which are wholly concerned with establishing a group in a particular milieu. For all the available data of groupwork problems point to the inescapable fact that ignoring such factors in no way lessens their influence on the group and its outcomes, it merely serves often enough to obfuscate the cause of problems and thus creates the possibility of the application of remedies almost certainly based on inaccurate diagnoses of the problem.

One final point relates to the assumption that groupwork is an economic use of valuable resources. *This is only true if the groupwork is effective.* Perhaps the real consideration should be the factor of time. Most estimates of economy in group use are based on the simple assessment of 'working with X clients in the time normally taken to work with one'. But such an assumption is based upon the fallacious assessment of the time necessary to achieve an *effective* outcome in a group. This is not a simple matter. Some groups can achieve a satisfactory outcome in one session having been refined to a design especially suited to the situation involved; others can take years. Within this continuum the usual assumptions of the 'economic' argument are far too small. Indeed I have much evidence of groups most inadequately completing the processes for which they were established because they were ended just when the unit/structure which would have been necessary for a successful completion was beginning to be established.

The unavoidable outcome of studying the problems of this chapter must be that groupworkers' professional skills need to be much wider in scope than the ability to establish a cosy relationship with a number of individuals in a given venue.

SECTIONAL REFERENCES

Organization and policy

Benson, J. F. (1987) *Working More Creatively With Groups*, London, Tavistock Publications.

Blau, P. M. and Scott, W. R. (1980) 'Who benefits', in A. Etzioni and E. W. Lehman (eds) *A Sociological Reader on Complex Organizations*, New York, Holt, Rinehart and Winston.

Time

El-Shamy, S. (1978) 'Small group assertion training: effects of time-spacing on outcomes', *Small Group Behavior* 9(3): 393–401, London, Sage Publications.

Size

Douglas, T. (1979) *Group Processes in Social Work*, Chichester, John Wiley and Sons, 87.

Hare, A. P. (1962) 'Group size', in *The Handbook of Small Group Research*, New York, Free Press of Glencoe, Chapter 8: 224–45.

Design

Garvin, C. D. (1981) *Contemporary Groupwork*, Englewood Cliffs, NJ, Prentice-Hall Inc., 78–9.

Glover, J. A. and Chambers, T. (1978) 'The creative production of the group: effects of structure', *Small Group Behavior* 9(3): 387–92, London, Sage Publications Ltd.

Hodge, J. (1977) 'Social groupwork – rules for establishing the group', *Social Work Today* 8(17): 8–11.

Kurland, R. (1978) 'Planning: the neglected component of group development', *Social Work with Groups* 1(2): 173–8, New York, The Haworth Press.

Weisberg, A. R. (1987) 'Single session group practice in a hospital', in J. Lassner, K. Powell and E. Finnegan (eds) *Social Group Work: Competence and Values in Practice*, New York, The Haworth Press, 104.

Chapter 6

Problems relating to the performance of leadership roles

GENERAL AREA OF PROBLEM

This, as one would expect, is by far the largest area of problems, quite simply because the vast majority of those who have contributed problems over the years have been those who work with groups. They are, with great justification, concerned with attempting to find some help with the problems and difficulties they encounter in their roles as leaders.

So here we have a large constellation of problems which are directly related to the creation, maintenance and use and termination of groups. It appears to divide into the following major categories:

A Those problems which appear to stem from the nature and quality of the groupworker's knowledge (theoretical or experiential) of groups and of the practice of groupwork.
B All those problems which relate to the practice of groupwork and which may be loosely classified as 'skills'.
C Another large category which falls generally under the rubric of leader performance and includes factors like style and role.
D The aims and objectives of leadership.

All those factors presented here relating to leadership skills and behaviour are the reverse side as it were of the problems in all the other chapters. This distinction is maintained here on the basis of how each problem was expressed, for example, all those problems which begin with 'How do I...?' are all leader problems in that they are a request for help from a leader in dealing with something he/she has come across in their groups and which can be expressed in terms of a problem or a difficulty (note – Category A, because it is concerned wholly with ideas, will need to be presented here in a manner structurally different from others, for example, it is wholly inappropriate to have a section on strategy).

A Those problems which appear to stem from the nature and quality of the groupworker's knowledge, theoretical and/or experiential, of groups and the practice of groupwork

Definition and comment

In essence this heading is self-defining. Many problems offered by practitioners eventually are seen to originate in a lack of some element of basic ideas about the ways in which human beings behave in groups.

Less frequently problems are presented in a way which clearly acknowledges that some essential knowledge may be lacking. In brief that lack may be of two kinds, one usually much more readily discussed than the other. This is the practice knowledge which is acquired by 'doing' groupwork or 'being' a member of a group and accumulating and reviewing such experiences. The other is material derived from research, literature and the consideration of theoretical concepts. The essential value of the latter is that it can and should provide a logically-related structure into which the experiential material can be slotted, especially if that structure does not have the restriction of being based purely or even largely on one and one only of the major approaches to the understanding of group behaviour. None have the merit of offering even an elegant theory or theories, let alone a complete one; all have the value that they add something to the total stock of knowledge. In an area of such diversity and complexity as group behaviour, even a few signposts which do not all point in the same direction can give a better understanding of the nature of the land-scape and the points of interest it contains.

But the idea that one form of knowledge can be used to create a structure to organize another more experiential form does not readily catch practitioners' attention, largely, one must admit, because the idea may never have been pre-sented as possessing much worth and also because the practicality and involvement of group situations does tend to encourage an exclusive and excluding immersion.

Examples of problems

'What type should we employ with a constantly changing population, do we look at group needs, group activities or variations of these and how do I marry this with the organizational needs and demands?'

'In helping a group to "gell" as soon as possible to begin work I need more information on the stages of formation to identify them and to be able to help the group through them.'

'I need to have a better understanding of group dynamics; how practical issues affect outcomes, for instance, and about different group models.'

'I need to know about leader behaviour in the sense of the knowledge-base upon which it is founded and its appropriateness to the task in hand.'

'Because I was trained to work with individuals I find it hard to make my interventions in the group – I would like to learn more about group process.'

'I would like information on working with or as a co-leader or a co-worker.'

'I need to develop further knowledge of intervention skills, that is, to know when to stop the group or not, when to intervene or not, and how to choose the appropriate action.'

'I need to acquire a wide knowledge-base of group skills by sharing with others techniques of approach, planning, implementation and evaluation.'

'I would like to explore different group models.'

Analysis of problems

The basic fact underlying the common problems sampled here is quite simply one of recognition of deficiency. The practitioners who stated these problems, and many others who made similar statements, are in effect saying that in certain acknowledged areas of their work with and in groups they have discovered that they do not have the basic knowledge to cope as effectively as they would like. Now this is so simple a statement that it cannot be wholly true and indeed it is not. There are those who may be possessed of the essential knowledge which they require in dealing with a current problem but who remain unaware of the connection between what they know and the problem which they face. Their knowledge is pigeon-holed in a different system from that of their practice. Others may know that certain theoretical concepts they possess are obviously relevant to the problems they have and yet be wholly unable to translate the former into practical strategies for dealing with the latter. In this context I would recommend practitioners to read Feldman's paper 'Determinants and objectives of social groupwork intervention' (1967: 34–57) for a clear method of the transformation of theoretical ideas of group behaviour into practical techniques of intervention.

Useful ideas

As this category is concerned almost exclusively with concepts this section will constitute the major presentation and is divided into two subsections. The first is concerned with ideas obtained from research and theory and the second is concerned with what, for want of a better term, might be designated as 'practice knowledge'.

1 Research material and theory

I think that there are two fundamental points to make here which may be stated quite baldly as

(a) teaching and learning on group behaviour which is most frequently found at the beginning of an individual's contact with groupwork, when in effect the ideas presented can be understood almost wholly as interesting abstractions. Their relationship to actually working with and being in the presence of significant others tends to be tenuous except for the fortune of accident. There is a very strong need for a thorough consideration of related theory and ideas to be entered into when practitioners have been in group or team-work long enough to realize not only that their basic underpinning of theory is deficient, but also to know quite clearly in what areas that deficiency exists. Theory then becomes clearly related to need and to obvious developmental progress.

(b) Without some knowledge of how one's practice is going the problems relating to deficient theoretical knowledge will not truly emerge or maybe they will emerge camouflaged as being the product of other factors. It becomes urgently necessary for development that problems should be located accurately in the exact area of causation. I have heard myself saying so often that the acknowledgement of ignorance is the beginning of wisdom, but I must admit that it is also essential that the ignorance which is acknowledged needs to be the 'real' basis of the problem. Once more the practitioner is faced with the need to keep some form of record of his/her work. It is not possible to ask for help in, say, understanding the stages of the formation of a group if the inability to help a group to 'gel' has not been located in that essential area of group behavioural knowledge.

2 Practice knowledge

This is, at its most basic, the information that practitioners record for the benefit of others, about the process of actually working in specific circumstances with a group or a team. Its advantages are that it is essentially a practical record related to 'real' experience; it deals with problems as they were encountered, with mistakes and consequences. Its focus is narrow and thus undiluted by wide general references. The disadvantages are exactly that the specificity creates a problem of transfer to other perhaps similar situations, frequently the sub-structure of theory which underpinned the whole exercise is not made clear; nor does the relationship of each bit of practice wisdom to every other bit emerge even tenuously, so the development of a coherent whole seldom becomes clear.

For these reasons practice knowledge keeps growing at an enormous rate but attempts to build up a more coherent structure from this mass of knowledge are inordinately scarce. The spin-off from this is that most contributions to group-work knowledge remain isolated and that practitioners continue to report experiences which remain markedly idiosyncratic and largely repetitive.

These two comments fall under the heading of 'useful ideas' which might with absolute justice be questionable as an apt description of them. But they are a necessary preliminary to the fundamental 'useful idea' in this category, which is the absolute need for every groupworker and team leader to construct, maintain and up-date his/her own personal reference library. Ideas which are culled from all sources, verbal, visual, experiential, because they strike a responsive chord, should be recorded along with the source. These ideas should then be tried out in practice and the consequences also recorded. The knowledge which is essential to the skilled practice with a group must in the end be a personal construction. It cannot be taken over as a prepared package from someone else because the essential element is the person who uses that knowledge and how he/she adapts it.

As we shall see later, the transfer of knowledge into practice is best performed in an apprenticeship system or in well-supervised practice. One thing is sure, that there is a great need for the actual skill of taking information and using it to design a strategy, to be more effectively learned. In some brief measure we have pursued the process of the translation of ideas into strategies throughout this book.

B Problems which relate to the practice of groupwork and which may be loosely classified as skill problems

Definition and comment

The larger part of all problems relate to skills in the practice of groupwork. How is it to be done? Naturally those who practise are aware that there are ways of doing quite ordinary things in a group context which although only slightly different in form, produce significantly different results. But this introduces an essential element of controversy between those who maintain that an increase in skill in handling or working with people equates with a diminution in sincerity in that a large part of the practice becomes a matter of the conscious use of learned techniques and those who say that the so-called 'natural' or 'instinctive' responses of the caring individual are insufficient. In the best of all worlds we would have both, and practitioners who knew when either or how much of each was an appropriate response to the needs of the group. But as adherence to either end of this continuum appears to be a matter of intensely personal and individual preference, and may in the long run be a matter of personality, few can be persuaded to examine their position objectively.

As the major position taken in this handbook is that underlying the development of skills there is the essential prerequisite of knowledge and understanding of the scale and structure of the large canvas upon which the techniques are but brush strokes. Skills and techniques when applied in the absence of, or defective nature of, this basic understanding are indeed little more than a bag of tricks. The danger of presenting just such a bag in a handbook like this is an omnipresent worry and it must be stressed the emphasis here is very much on the development of a skill of recognition, and analysis of problems which is then developed into the design of appropriate strategies firmly founded in the wide understanding of group behaviour and the effective methods of strategy design.

Examples of problems

'How do I help the timid members?'

'How do I translate experience into leader skill?'

'How do I translate thinking to action?'

'How do I acquire the skill of intervention?'

'How do I deal with silences?'

'How do I draw members out?'

'How do I create the right atmosphere?'

'How do I understand what is being said, or being presented as non-verbal communication?'

'How do I use language, the form of words as a leader skill?'

'How do I get information disseminated completely and accurately?'

'I am unsure of the techniques and relative importance of the various aspects of people's lives that need to be focused on in the group.'

'How do I get the group to impose a degree of control?'

'How best to achieve termination in groups?'

'How do I use video equipment to best advantage in groups?'

'How do I develop a greater sense of perception as to "underlying" elements within a group which are not immediately obvious to external observation?'

'How do I overcome the combined effects of strong peer-group loyalty and lack of self-confidence to encourage individuals to comment on the group and to interact?'

'How do I allow members freedom of interpretation whilst at the same time keeping to previously agreed boundaries?'

'How do I create a group identity?'

'How do I maintain control of 16- to 17-year-olds?'

'How do I plan a group in advance when I know I will have to reassess the direction being taken when the group actually meets?'

'How do I handle disruptive behaviour?'

'I need to "polish-up" my skills in the area of offering structure/framework for decision-making without imposing decisions on group members.'

'How do I acquire the skills of intervention – getting the group started, listening, intervening, coping with a long silence.'

'How do I draw out and motivate the quiet and introverted members?'

'How do I provide an atmosphere/environment for a group of adults which does not resemble a schoolroom and an adult/pupil relationship?'

'How do I encourage a group spirit and identity?'

'How do I develop the skills to make discussions constructive and interesting?'

'How do I plan for a group?'

'The difficulties I encounter are – starting the group.
                                   – coping with aggression.
                                   – dealing with some of the
                                       more disruptive members.
                                   – finishing the group.'

' I need skills in presenting, constructing and analysing groupwork.'

'How do I involve members in decision-making which they try to opt out of and make them aware of the way the leaders resolve their differences of opinion and approach?'

'How do I involve members of my Intermediate Treatment group in discussions so that everybody participates?'

'How do I acquire the techniques to deal with group conflict and how do I learn ways to deal with that conflict at the appropriate time rather than intellectualizing/rationalizing to avoid coping with it?'

'How can I introduce new members to an established group – make them feel welcome and at the same time build on what has gone before?'

'How do I end a group, ensuring that the work to be done has been completed in the allotted time span, and that individual members are not left in the air when the group is finished?'

Analysis of problems

I think it must be all too obvious from the foregoing that a large proportion of problems are presented as skill deficiences which is not at all surprising when we consider that operating in or with a group is a complex social skill. I have just one cavil to make here which is that social skill has as a large constituent, and very important part, a sensitivity to, and understanding of, the social context in which it may be needed. Thus although learning under instruction on the basis of trial and error, those actual behaviours which are ubiquitously called skills are never enough. What also needs to be learned is to recognize the situation in which they may be appropriately applied and the form in which they might best be offered. Unfortunately the context most favourable to acquiring this skill-related sensitivity is that of supervised practice. But what I can offer here is a series of guidelines for the development of some of the skills so urgently requested by those who proffered the problems quoted here. What is at issue is the ability to use the essentials of the problem to locate and develop a method of dealing with it.

Strategies

If you are asking a question of the nature of 'How do I do this or that?' then there are certain procedures to follow which should help to answer the question when outside and/or experienced help is not available. Let us take first a simple example and then later one of much greater complexity.

Example A 'How do I help the timid members?'

(a) Let us assume that the statement that some members of a group are timid is correct and that also being timid they really do need help (both these points can be verified beyond the state of being mere assumptions on the basis of observed behaviour; by gentle discussion with the so-called 'timid' members outside of the group).
(b) Consider the nature of timidity – in most instances it amounts to a fear of being placed in a position of high visibility, of the unacceptably high risk position of being made to look and feel foolish or ridiculous usually associated with a low level of self-esteem and/or long-standing hurtful experiences of just such situations which has caused the development of a protective and defensive avoidance of situations which are perceived as containing the elements of potential threat of exposure.
(c) Having clarified the nature of the problem the next step is to ask what kind of action or behaviour might serve directly or indirectly to change the essential perception of threat and reduce the element of fear.

Direct comment is usually counter-productive – it only highlights what the timid want to remain hidden.

But there are three techniques which are usually only confounded by the most abnormal of fears or lack of self-esteem of a pathological order:

(i) By example – every time it becomes necessary to inform group members that they can say what they want, then the more verbal members should be encouraged to yield space and time to those less able to make their points by virtue of their timidity – indeed it should be made clear that such members will be protected as of right when they wish to speak, especially if some sign of intent to speak can be agreed upon in advance. This takes time which may not be available but it has the advantage that it creates the growing perception in the timid that some element of safety exists in the group and that this they can observe for themselves.

(ii)   By discovering what, if any, resource timid members may have which may be of value to the group and feeding this with great sensitivity into the group. This has the potential of generating increased regard for these members and thus to counter one of the basic elements of timidity which is a low self-esteem.

Interestingly this technique highlights the usual inadequacy of the information we tend to have about group members. This problem is dealt with elsewhere in this book (see Chapter 3), and it is often difficult to observe and use resources in this way.

(iii)   By practical coaching in the art of 'getting in' which may take the form of role play or of direct interplay between timid member and group leader with a great deal of protection and encouragement involved.

Incidentally, I find it quite discouraging that such a number of groupworkers find the idea unusual that members of a group may have to be taught gently and persuasively the basic techniques of working within a group. If the most powerful asset of a group is the resources to which it has access, then members who cannot commit what resources they have to the common good, by virtue of the lack of basic skills of group contribution, are deprived of acceptance and the group's ability thereby diminished. Where it is felt possible the group's whole-hearted assistance may be used to deal with the problem of the timid member, but until some degree of willingness on the part of the timid member to submit to this has been obtained it must be borne in mind that using the group in this way involves a fairly rapid increase in exposure for the timid member.

The basic steps then are: statement of the problem; clarification of its essential components; development of ideas specifically concerned to ameliorate the effects of one or more of the essential components; putting the ideas into practice with care and sensitivity being mindful of the consequences foreseen and unforeseen and monitoring them with care.

Example B 'How do I handle disruptive behaviour – group conflict?'

At the very beginning of discussing strategies it is necessary to make one or two points clear:

1 Conflict and 'disruptive behaviour' are natural parts of social behaviour.
2 They both generate and use considerable resources of energy.

3 The term 'disruptive' is a description of the effect of certain kinds of be haviour from one particular point of view.
4 'Disruptive' behaviour seen from the point of view of the 'disruptor' may be an extremely credible behavioural pattern.
5 Very few people make an absolute hobby of being 'bloody-minded' and hostility and destruction for sheer pleasure are indeed very rare.
6 There are 'independents' and 'rebels' in most groups – their behaviour can be extremely valuable but it can also be destructive.

Ideas for handling 'disruptive behaviour'

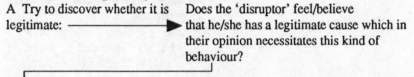

A Try to discover whether it is   Does the 'disruptor' feel/believe
legitimate: ─────────────▶ that he/she has a legitimate cause which in
                              their opinion necessitates this kind of
                              behaviour?

If it is, then it is necessary to try to elicit what that legitimate cause might be – which does not mean asking 'Why do you do this?' but rather attempting to discover what end the behaviour is trying to achieve.

This is difficult because the field of legitimacy may include several major areas:

1 Causes which stem from the individual's presence in the group, for example:

   (a) the response to others;
   (b) the response from others.

2 Causes which are imported, for example:

   (a) bad feelings towards situations and/or people outside the group but which are expressed within the group having no real relationship to it or its work;
   (b) similar – but feelings are related to events within the group and are easily misunderstood to be caused by it.

3 The method of expression, that is, 'disruption', is:

   (a) based on past experience as a successful way of dealing with the disruptor's problems;
   (b) is part of a characteristic response.

Where legitimacy is established the next step is to establish consciousness of consequence and if possible intention: ————————————————➤ In essence this means accepting the right of the individual to express his/her cause but equally maintaining the right to question the way in which it is being expressed by:

(a) demonstrating the apparent consequences of the behaviour to the group and
(b) asking if these consequences are what was intended or merely a largely unforeseen byproduct

If intended...
Then there is a need to establish the legitimacy of the individual's right to cause this outcome in the group.

If not intended...
Then there is a need to establish other methods of allowing the individual expression of his/her legitimate feelings.

Then it is necessary to address the complaint which motivates the 'disruptive' behaviour – because while it exists unresolved, much energy will be diverted from the group task to deal with it.

This implies a demonstration/teaching/learning situation with the whole group or with the individual in the context of the group.

Acceptable adjustment is the goal,

Methods: discussion; example; role play, simulation, and so on.

or if the cost is too high – departure of the 'disruptive' member.

Legitimacy of 'disruption' is a difficult concept because it depends upon priority – as a rule of thumb it is better to accept that all 'disruption' is a legitimate expression until there is evidence to the contrary. Thus the strategies for dealing with 'disruption' tend to centre, not so much round the legitimacy of the cause but rather the consequences of the expression.

Legitimacy of behaviour of group members is based upon one thing: *that it promotes the agreed aims of the group either currently or in the long term.* Promotive behaviour may occur in any or all of three areas:

(a) In promoting the working of the group as a unit, that is, developing appropriate co-operation, trust, in creating methods, roles, patterns, and so on.
(b) Generating a level of personal safety appropriate to the commitment of personal resources.
(c) Actually facilitating the performance of those tasks for which the group was created.

Long-term consequences are very difficult to determine.

B Non-legitimate disruption – that is disruption which is discovered –

(a) to stem from outside of the group and which is of no legitimate concern to the group.

The strategy should be to attempt to provide help to deal with the problem outside the group which will enable the member to remain as an active and involved contributor to the group process.

(b) to cause the group to be unable to pursue its own agreed goals.

The strategy should be to remove the person from the group with the offer of an alternative form of assistance.

(c) to be a pattern of expression which cannot be modified sufficiently to be contained within the group's process.

The strategy should be expulsion from the group.

If the basic reason for the creation and use of a group is to gain access to and use of resources which exist both actually and in potential within it, then individual behaviour which diminishes or prevents the fulfilment of this purpose has to be considered very seriously. Ultimately the success of the group process has to have a higher priority than any individual member except for those periods when the group is being used as an instrument of treatment for one member. This is then part of the group's accepted work pattern and is contained and controlled within its general process.

(d) to stem from personal circumstances with which the group has no mandate or no ability to cope, for example:
- essentially disturbed, or
- disorientated behaviour, or
- malicious intent, for example, bullying.

The strategy should be to exclude from the group but with the offer of assistance if acceptable, or if not able to contain, to exclude from the group.

C Status – the response to 'disruptive' behaviour has been noted to vary according to the group's perception of the status of the 'disruptor'. Thus high status members who are known to provide good things for the group are often allowed more frequent and/or more intense episodes of disruption than those members whose contribution to the group is ordinary (the so-called 'idiosyncrasy credits' (Hollander 1960)).

The strategy here is that of containment based on the expressed and known value of the high status member – 'this is a cost we pay for what we know we will get later'. If the 'goods' do not arrive of course then the cost has to be reconsidered.

D Persistence – Incidents of 'disruption' will occur anyway – persistent 'disruption' may reduce legitimacy and thus bring into consideration some of the factors noted here.

Useful references to a great deal of matter concerned with disruptive behaviour can be found in the literature under 'deviance from norms' and under 'conflict'.

Disruptive behaviour can serve a positive function in that it tends to force clarification in the group about what it is about and what its norms are (see, for instance, Dentler and Erikson 1959).

E Independence – defined by Napier and Gershenfeld (1973:91) as 'indifference to the normative expectations of other people and groups'.

The strategy here is to attempt to use as much of the independence as possible for the benefit of the group and to contain the rest. This is more easily achieved when the independent member has high status within the group (see above).

Summary   In this example the stage of clarification is essentially very complicated because the causative factors underlying 'disruptive' behaviour can be extremely varied. The understanding required to initiate a strategy to cope with it has to be acquired from (a) existing knowledge from all available sources, and (b) by eliciting information from group members, and (c) by direct but sensitive enquiry, and (d) by observation.

One final note about high status members – Sabath (1964) discovered that group members tended to discount the misbehaviour of high status members, whereas with members of ordinary status disruptive behaviour had to be followed by behaviour that had a favourable outcome for the group before they would forgive the disruptors.

This would serve to indicate that a possible strategy would be to ensure that the full value of the disruptive member to the group ought to be emphasized so that it could ameliorate their reaction.

C Leader performance including style and role

Definition and comment

The perfomance of leadership tasks within a group situation has ultimately to be finely adjusted to the kind of person each individual leader happens to be. Performance may be measured in terms of how successful or otherwise a leader is in enabling his/her groups to achieve their desired goals, whether these be the achievement of specific tasks, or more in the nature of the development of the group as a social unit, or in the personal growth of its members. But whatever style of leadership is assumed, that style must sit in harmony with the person who is the leader and must, above all, be an asset to the group in which it is practised.

So it becomes necessary to define what may be called 'personal' leadership styles and roles in distinction to what, I suppose, can be referred to as the 'general' leadership style, that is, those which are expressions of particular ideas or theories of behaviour or even philosophy. Thus the style known as 'directive' can be a personal style or one based on concepts which require this form of approach or can be founded on a leader's ability to produce a directive style when he/she believes it is necessary either for a particular group or at a particular time in the life of a group. Ultimately a directive style may be founded on a philosophy which would indicate that people only grow and learn under firm controlling and knowledgeable direction. And so it is with other approaches to the performance of leadership roles.

Examples of problems

'I start to question myself as to whether I am suited to this particular type of group – this occurs amongst other staff also who are not particularly open about their views which leads to suspicion and an atmosphere which is counterproductive to sharing.'

'There are problems of co-working, for example, working with a more experienced worker brings up the problem of the dual role learner and leader of achieving a balance between male/female worker's role – the selection of a colleague or other to work with as co-leader – how to achieve a balance of power between professionals and volunteers as leaders – of the leader becoming immersed in the group and dominating the proceedings and thus not leaving space for the contributions of the co-worker – the need for staff to be prepared for co-working – where should individual differences between staff co-workers be settled, in or out of the group? – how can disagreements between co-leaders on decisions be communicated to the group?'

'My personal style is to become fairly central as a leader and I can find myself interacting too much with one client at a time rather than facilitating and stimulating the group members' interaction with each other.'

'I find that I need to give group members more space but I know I must avoid making myself and others anxious by a lack of structure and input.'

'There is a problem of choosing group leaders who can cope – what are the ways of working together and what styles should we look for?'

'How can I steer the group in a positive direction without taking over total leadership?'

'How can I deal with confrontations and use it as an effective technique?'

'I feel I have a responsibility for other people – I talk for others when it could be more appropriate to help them to talk for themselves.'

'I am uncomfortable when the group is taking on a "feeling" level and as a result I want to move on to solutions.'

'I wish to learn how and when to stand back and hand over to my co-worker.'

'How much interaction should there be between co-therapists in a group?'

Analysis of problems

The problems presented here seem to accumulate around five points:

1 Sharing the leadership role with others, for example, co-working, volunteers.
2 The position of leader *vis-à-vis* the group, for example, dominant, central, peripheral.
3 The creation of structure.
4 Responsibility for the group.
5 Blind spots.

Useful ideas

As leadership, its forms, styles, theories, and so on, is one of the areas of group-work with the most massive amount of literature, indicating no doubt that it is an area of central concern, the number of concepts and ideas relating even to just the five areas mentioned above is legion. I will endeavour to be selective.

Shared leadership	The ideas here range from the simple concept that two leaders cover the two major areas of group need, thus one is task-oriented and one concerned with the maintenance of the group, to those concepts like democracy (of paramount importance in self-help groups) where leadership is a function of the whole group.
Techniques of shared leadership	There are many relevant ideas about co-working in groups which go all the way from sharing in what amounts to the leadership subgroup with equals, to the use of the co-leadership system as a means of training (see Chapter 7).
Social power	In social situations power tends to be given to people or invested in them based on the giver's perception. If that perception changes then it is likely that the ascription of power will change also.
Developmental sequence	At different periods within the life of a group the kind of leadership that it will require will change. The most marked points of the sequence are the beginning and end of a group and of course crisis points during its life. The required leadership activity may not always come from the officially designated leader.
The possibility of the interchangeability of relationships and structure	All groups have some structure, in some it is almost wholly the structure of relationships – this has a degree of fragility which can be shattered – a more formal structure of roles is a more lasting edifice, but circum-

stances sometimes dictate that one must be substituted for the other.

Visibility

Leaders are usually highly visible – their actions are more likely to be accepted as a true representation of what they stand for than their words – if the group's aim is to learn how to take responsibility for itself, then constant behaviour by the leader which indicates that he/she arrogates to him/herself responsibility, then visibility will ensure inhibition of the group's development.

Blind spots

(see Jo-Harri Window in Luft 1963). Most of us are unaware of some of our deficiencies but they are often clearly visible to others – feedback is the tool by which they become known.

Self-awareness

A widely-used term but one which can usefully be boiled down to representing a reasonably clear idea about how we present to others and implying an acceptance that if that is the way we are seen, then it will dictate the manner of the response of others to us whether we like it or not.

Of course there are many other ideas about leadership, for example, status, physical presence, verbal skills, observational ability, and so on, most of which are presented in the literature. Some sources will be given in the references at the end of this chapter.

Strategies

Leadership is defined by Napier and Gershenfeld (1973) as 'which style or combination of styles will help the group arrive at its goals consistent with the values of that organization?' (p.160).

The principal strategies in this area are indeed quite few:

1 Learn the range of leadership styles.
2 Learn in what kind of situations particular styles are most effective.
3 Learn which particular styles are compatible with you as a person and group leader.
4 Exercise only those you feel competent and confident to practise.

1 Leadership styles

The main continuum of leader style is usually defined as from Leader centred – Group centred.

Action – read pages 158–65 of Napier and Gershenfeld, or Thomas Gordon's paper on the 'Group-centred leader' in Diedrich and Dye's (1972: 71–101) *Group Procedures, Purposes, Processes and Outcomes.*

The Napier and Gershenfeld contribution is particularly useful in that it relates in quite simple form group conditions to appropriate leadership style.

2 Group situations or conditions

Action – see above.

Read also 'A broad range model of practice in the social-work group' by Norma Lang (1972) in which she describes the leader response appropriate to a variety of group conditions:

Example 1 of the adaptation of leadership style to the presenting conditions. A group has the following conditions:

(i)   A strictly limited and short time in which to operate, which cannot be changed.
(ii) The task is to provide a decision – a fact which is known and understood by the group members.
(iii) The group members are known to possess potentially adequate resources to complete the task.
(iv) The members are known to each other.

Then the appropriate leadership style would contain:

(i)   A large element of direction and control.
(ii) Considerable reviewing procedures involving recapitulation.

The reasons for this choice of style are as follows:

(a) The task is known, clear and unambiguous.
(b) The time allotted to the task is set.
(c) What is required is that the members should concentrate on the matter in hand:

 – that the nature of the task and the conditions and the form of group operation required to meet them is spelled out with absolute clarity at the start of the group and agreed on if only for the period under consideration.
 – that each member should have a ration of space and time compatible with being a fair share of that allowed for the task.
 – that each member should be held to that form of material which would be necessary in the making of the essential decisions and prevented from wandering, elaborating or other animadversions or from introducing interesting but otherwise irrelevant material.

The leader needs periodically to collect together and present what material has already been acquired and to control the time when it is appropriate to consider what evidence there is for making a decision, and to stop the group when that decision is reached at a point within the allotted span.

The style of leadership absolutely essential in this situation is thus described as directive, task-oriented, time-limited with maximum concern for tapping the available resources and using them.

Example 2   Lang (1972) offered the following kind of correlationship between the situation of group members and leadership style:

Group members	*Leadership style*
A Lack experience and the capacity and skill to use the group efficiently.	Directive – 'aims to supply the missing pieces in the group process'.
B Have potential capacity and skill.	Variable between directive and facilitative.
C Capable and skilled in group functioning.	Facilitative.

3 Personal compatibility

This can only be achieved by trying things out:

(a) First, whether an idea sits comfortably in mind or not as a form of leadership.
(b) Obtain feedback from others, colleagues and group members about the variety of styles used.
(c) Examine closely one's own feelings about the way in which leadership acts felt while being performed.
(d) Record carefully those areas deemed compatible for future reference.
(e) Every so often review one's performance and development as a groupworker.

4 Competent practice

Most of the above is relevant here also.

D The aims and objectives of leadership

Definition and comment

The essential objective of leadership must be to promote two sets of aims – those which the leader has for the group, and those which the group has set for itself (which may be different). The apparent discrepancy here is often more apparent than real. For example, the group may have as its basic aim the need to support its members in their confrontation with some sort of authority. The group leader, while obviously having this as his/her long-term purpose also, has other, probably more urgent, goals which require him/her to help the group weld itself into a unit which can act to achieve the important aim for which it was set up. The disparity of aims may reside almost entirely in the different perceptions of leader and group about preparation, support systems, actual needs, and so on, based upon a more comprehensive understanding of group processes and the methods of working with them; assets more usually possessed by a group leader.

Examples of problems

'How should I deal with the problem of achieving personal work goals in a group in a setting where there are different priorities?'

'How do I set appropriate aims and objectives for clients of a social work agency matching my expectations to theirs whilst still providing a medium for growth and learning?'

'How does one deal with hidden agendas?'

'I have a problem finding common ground – developing an appropriate starting point which adequately sets out the goals of the group whilst at the same time motivating interest.'

'How do I define the aims of groups more clearly?'

'How much is group-motivation dependent upon the relationship between members and group leaders?'

Analysis of problems

It is noticeable in the problems stated that there is a clear identification of the multiplicity of goals/aims which can exist in even the simplest group (see Chapter 3, category A4).

Fundamentally, the aim of effective leadership must be to enable any group to develop the ability to achieve the ends for which it was established or to discover that, for whatever reason, such ends are not possible. This boils down to the following essentials:

1 Helping, guiding and encouraging group members to develop as the kind of unit which can most effectively achieve its ends having first established what those ends might be.
2 Discover, make visible and allow for, other goals which are in existence within the group and calculate what effect if any they might have on the overall achievement of the group and its members as individuals.

3 Use such knowledge of group behaviour as is available to encourage the group to make choices.
4 Provide a basic sense of security and expert resourcefulness (expert, that is, in the way groups can work).

Even if the leader is working in the extreme way with individuals in the context of the group and the basic structure is formed by the similarity of the relationship each individual member has to the leader, the essential aims listed above are valid.

There are subsidiary aims relating to learning through doing and to obtaining a sufficient modicum of satisfaction. There may also be aims which relate to the philosophy and training of the individual groupworker and those of the employing organization to which the groupworker subscribes.

Useful ideas

I think it should be stated here that to attempt to offer a series of strategies for the development of leadership objectives would be a fairly useless exercise. So I have put down those ideas which should be most useful for the reader in forming his/her own aims and objectives. In essence they are all concerned with the development of a clear understanding of what the individual leader has to offer, squaring this with what the potential group members need and what they have to offer and making an agreement to engage in a process of working together.

The complexity of the groupwork task	Groupwork is not a soft option – each group is a microcosm of life and can be just as complicated – the recognition that this is so must underlie whatever objectives a groupworker has for him/herself and for the group.
Leadership continuum	There are obviously going to be places on the continuum where an individual worker feels essentially confident and comfortable and there will be others which are frightening or at least uncomfortable and difficult. Whatever objective a leader sets for him/herself must be within or on the edges of those known areas. Otherwise the leader is offering to potential members to accept in good faith what in fact it may not be possible to deliver.
Personal clarity	This has some of the elements of self-awareness about it but is directly concerned with the understanding of: (a) The position the leader occupies *vis-à-vis* the group members.

(b) The standing the leader is accorded.

(c) What precisely the leader is trying to do.

Visibility

This has been covered elsewhere, but when leadership objectives are being established it does no harm to remember that the main factor by which leader-worth is assessed is performance and especially the compatibility with stated intent that it demonstrates.

Contract

Also discussed elsewhere, but it serves to reinforce the point that objectives can only be set realistically by people who know what is available to become part of the offer.

Total scene

One of the main objectives of leadership should be to become aware of the total scene in which the group operates any part of which may seriously affect the group's outcomes. Groups can be such absorbing situations that tunnel vision with regard to the total scene can easily develop and as a result situations develop as surprises which might have been anticipated.

Feedback

To be constantly accessible to feedback about performance is essential to development and may be the sole most important factor in refining objectives to a more realistic model.

Power

Power is usually accorded, probably by those who have a perception that it already exists. Leadership objectives should include a recognition that this is so and develop a satisfactory method of using it to the advantage of the group and probably developing the group's recognition of and ability to use its own power.

Communication

All groupwork leaders must have as part of their equipment the ability to communicate which includes the ability to receive communications.

The problems stated at the beginning of this section could be seen as admissions of a lack of certain skills but equally they are statements about uncertainty of the aims and objectives of leadership in particular situations. How is it possible for instance to set out clear goals for a group when one of the principal means of achieving any goal is a clear knowledge on the part of the worker of the part he or she can play in achieving them?

Most certainly one of the greatest factors for engendering faith in a leader, any leader not just in groupwork, is a perception of their competence. Granted that it may be badly judged but I have heard so many group members say 'We got off to a good start because we all felt he/she knew what he/she was doing'.

DISCUSSION

A fact which has for many years come frequently to mind during my discussions with groupworkers has been how little attention most of them seem to have given to what can be called the milieu in which their groups exist. Groupworkers devote enormous energy and enthusiasm to working with a group but the very energy that is committed seems to diminish the little attention paid to the surroundings of the group. I have often been told that the task of the groupworker is to work with a group or groups which by implication inferred that anything else was not to be considered as part of the essential leadership task. But it should be.

Many of the problems arise because there are conflicts and contradictions inherent between the form of group which is created and the systems and surroundings in which it is located. But because small attention has been paid to them the system and surroundings are seldom adduced as the source of problems occurring within the group. This is sad because much energy is thereby diverted from productive work with the group, into pursuing causes of problems within the group, when in actuality they are outside it and are often not readily subject to change and should have formed an essential part of the original group design.

It must be obvious also in this section that I believe groups should be created to meet the needs of their members and the aims and objectives of the systems in which they are located. Which means that groupworkers and team leaders should have a range of leadership styles and skills which will enable them to create and operate groups specifically to meet those needs. It is still common practice that potential members are squeezed into that particular or limited group form which comprises the repertoire of the groupworker, whatever their actual needs. With a limited and similar potential member population from which to draw this may be a very successful ploy but most of us do not work to such well-defined and similar populations and thus a wide range of possibilities is essential if we are not to become 'Procrustean' groupworkers.

Finally I would like to offer an example of the leader's ability to assess the condition of a group and thus decide the appropriate response.

Example

A groupworker talking about a group which had been in existence for several years and which had just gone through a fairly tough phase, for example, complaining about its handling by the management of a social work authority, losing its groupworker, and so on, expressed surprise at the way he had been received as the replacement groupworker. The group's reputation was a tough one, critical, demanding and hard. His expectations had been set up by this reputation and he admitted to feeling uncomfortable with the calm even warm and friendly reception he had received. Was he being set up so he could be knocked down? When was the fuse going to blow?

The groupworker was talking in terms of 'the group had *lost* its groupworker'. But other workers in the service knew that this particular group had never really liked its groupworker. The fact that his colleagues accepted him as a highly-skilled, knowledgeable and competent worker had only served to blind them to the response he had provoked in his group. His going was no *loss* to his group but a positive gain.

Also the replacement groupworker was a worker who had created a good impression with his group in the same system and their opinion carried weight with their colleagues. Thus his new group already had pleasant expectations before his arrival based on an information source that they were prepared to trust.

Then despite the sequence of apparent disasters in the brief period immediately prior to the replacement groupworker arriving, there had also been a fairly huge influx of satisfaction for the group members. Thus the system had started to pay dividends after a longish period when little had occurred that was positive.

The balance of satisfactions in this group when most factors were taken into account came down fairly clearly on the positive side and may well have been the reason why the replacement worker was so amicably received. How tragic it would have been if his own expectations of the group based upon a true, but biased sample of their behaviour, had led him to respond not only with puzzlement, but with an anticipation of hostility and rough treatment. His suspicious approach might well have precipitated just the response he expected and produced a self-fulfilling prophecy.

Another truism emerges from this example which is that our assessments of situations are only equal to the quality and quantity of our understanding of the complex interacting network of systems which promoted them.

SECTIONAL REFERENCES

A

Feldman, R. A. (1967) 'Determinants and objectives of social groupwork intervention', in J. L. Roney (ed.) *Social Work Practice*, New York, Columbia University Press.

Northen, J. (1987) 'Selection of groups as the preferred modality of practice', in J. Lassner, K. Powell and E. Finnegan (eds) *Social Groupwork: Competence and Values in Practice*, New York, The Haworth Press, Chapter 2.

Reid, K. (1988) 'But I don't want to lead a group': some common problems of social workers leading groups', *Groupwork* 1(2): 124, London, Whiting and Birch.

B

Hollander, E. P. (1960) 'Competence and conformity in the acceptance of influence', *Journal of Abnormal and Social Psychology* 61: 365–8.

Sabath, G. (1964) 'The effect of disruption and individual status on person perception and group attraction', *Journal of Social Psychology* 64 (first half): 119–30.

C

Dentler, R. A. and Erikson, K. T. (1959) 'The function of deviance in groups', *Social Problems* III(2): 98–107.

Gordon, T. (1972) 'Group-centred leadership', in R. C. Diedrich and H. A. Dye (eds) *Group Procedures, Purposes, Processes and Outcomes*, Boston, Houghton Mifflin.

Lang, N. C. (1972) 'A broad range model of practice in the social-work group', *The Social Service Review* 46(1): 76–89.

Luft, J. (1963) The Jo–Harri Window is to be found in *Group Processes: An Introduction to Group Dynamics*, Palo Alto, Calif., National Press, 10–15.

Napier, R. N. and Gershenfeld, M K. (1973) *Groups: Theory and Experience*, Boston, Houghton Mifflin, 91 ff.

D

French, J. R. P. and Raven, B. (1959) 'The bases of social power', in M. D. Cartwright (ed.) *Studies in Social Power*, University of Michigan, Ann Arbor, Institute for Social Research, 150–67.

Chapter 7

Problems relating to the supervision, training and development of groupworkers

GENERAL AREA OF PROBLEM

One result of the growing interest in groupwork has naturally been a proliferation of groupwork problems relating to the supervision and training of groupworkers. Thus supervisors find themselves responsible for the development of students practising a complex 'people-handling' skill which was not a major part of their own professional training.

Moreover, when this is not so there still remains the ordinary problem of having the skills of training and supervising which are notoriously different from those of actual practice. While I have stated this difference baldly, there are many mitigating factors. For instance, supervision of groupworkers can be done on a group basis and the experience of that particular group used as a powerful learning situation.

The feelings that students have in arriving in a learning group can be illuminating about the similar feelings that group members have in other groups whose principal objective is not learning about groups. So a large number of problems have arisen based on how it may be possible to recognize and deal with the feelings of arrival in a learning group; about the recognition of the stages of skill development; ways in which the group leader's role changes in this sort of group – particularly in relation to being a group facilitator, but also the assessor of progress towards acquiring a 'licence to practise'; the analysis of the learning of members and many other factors which occur when the group does not comprise a membership which can be seen as 'clients'.

This can provide a great deal of learning about attitudes and the essential nature of working with human beings rather than a class of problems or difficulties. People are people first, and only second are they probationers, elderly, frail or delinquent.

Although it would be possible to include these problems elsewhere, for example under 'leadership' or even under 'members', the somewhat peculiar nature of the training relationship deserves special consideration. A simple dichotomy between trainers/teachers/supervisors and the roles of student/learner/apprentice provide the two basic categories:

A Problems which are presented by those in the trainer/teacher/supervisor role, and

B Problems presented by and concerned with those in the student/learner/ apprentice role.

A Problems presented by those in the trainer/teacher/supervisor role

Definition and comment

There is in reality no definition of this area of problems because they are multivariate. Basically they are problems which inhere in any teaching/learning situation where the ultimate achievement is a highly-complex interpersonal relationship skill which is founded upon a wide range of theoretical material. Thus problems are concerned with the transfer of learning, particularly from the classroom situation to actually working with people in groups; with the selection of those who should receive training and supervision; with the assessment of performance, and so on. But above all these matters is that relating to the method of teaching and learning groupwork which involves being a member of a group, usually with the express task of classifying group behaviour, in which the teacher is also the group leader. In itself this is an excellent way to learn, but it does become problematic when such a learning system is locked into an assessment system which is related in turn directly to some form of qualification to practise. Another fairly troubling situation arises when teachers, supervisors and assessors, who have themselves little or no groupwork expertise or practice, find themselves having to support, encourage and make decisions about groupwork students. Even the assessment of progress by results is fraught with difficulty as well-designed instruments to measure change are not readily available or markedly objective when they are. Indeed it may well be the way in which something is done in a group which has the major, usually immeasureable, effect and is the criterion of success, rather than the more obvious 'what' has been done.

Examples of problems

'How do I identify people who should be a part of the group?'

'What standards are there for assessing students who run groups? How do we supervise this?'

'How do you encourage people to talk in a group?'

'What is the role of a group leader who is also teacher/supervisor?'

'How do we encourage students to challenge control? Is this appropriate?'

'How does one prevent the group leader becoming the focus of the group?'

'How does one help a "stuck" group?'

'How do we assess what is happening in groups?'

'How do we analyse the learning which comes from being in groups?'

'What do you do about scapegoating?'

'How do we take the magic out of groupwork and turn the myths into facts, information and skills?'

'Where can one get support to say "No"?'

'A major problem is concerned with switching roles.'

'What is the balance between individual and group need?'

'How do you assess the quality of a group experience?'

'What happens when the group ends?'

'How do we deal with students with physical handicaps like hearing impairment?'

'What effects does fatigue cause?'

'What qualities does one need to be a group "leader" rather than an "enabler" or "facilitator"?'

'I need to develop further the ability to verbalize group skills to enable myself to begin to learn and pass on to co-workers basic groupwork skills – to know how to pass on and what when the co-workers are at different levels of understanding of groupwork, and deciding on the appropriate method of doing this.'

'Where can I get the information and criteria to help me judge when an initially inexperienced co-worker can take on more, and ultimately full, responsibility for the group?'

'Groupwork is learned by doing. I feel it is important to be able to offer my students a wider variety of models and skills.'

'Are group supervision techniques an extension of individual supervision processes?'

Analysis of problems

The problem material here appears to break down into seven major areas:

1 How can potential groupworkers be selected?
2 How can standards of assessment of what is happening, of the amount and quality of learning be arrived at?

3 In the teaching situation what are the methods of encouraging; of demystification of groupwork; developing challenge and the techniques of presentation and of making a rational decision between the needs of the group and of the individual?
4 What should be the role of the teacher/supervisor given that there is a frequent need to switch roles and the great likelihood of being cast as the group's focal point?
5 In a learning group how are the common group problems such as being stuck, scapegoating and termination dealt with?
6 How can support for teacher/supervisor(s) be provided?
7 How can the problems of physical handicap and fatigue be dealt with?

It must be obvious that a great number of the problems presented here have their counterparts in problems offered under other headings elsewhere in this book. And it would be true to say that the learning/teaching system under which these problems arise is not a difference of absolute distinction from the other problems. In all groupwork situations there is a greater or lesser element of learning and, of course, of teaching and supervising. The major difference must therefore lie in the fact that the learning/teaching problems addressed here are those which arise in the context of the group, being, or about to become, groupwork practitioners. What students learn in these situations will most certainly form the basis of their practice with their clients, although it may well be modified even quite drastically in the light of experience. I would suggest that this fact sharpens the sense of responsibility of those involved quite markedly.

Useful ideas

Signalling	Changes of role can be essentially very confusing when they occur in people who are seen as possessing considerable power by those who may believe they themselves possess little. Thus any change should be clearly signalled verbally and whatever definition is given to any role should be completely supported by the behaviour and performance within it.
Groupwork potential	Some people appear to have a natural ability to work with groups, others appear to be frightened by the very idea – in my experience neither are very sure indicators of the eventual level of groupwork skill that will emerge. There is no substitute for watching, monitoring and supervising potential groupworkers' progress over quite a period of time in making an effective assessment. What is just as important is that all who are interested should be allowed to try, and

second, that it should be possible to direct learners into those levels of groupwork skill wherein they show promise rather than expect an even development across the whole range.

Assessment standards

At rock bottom these have to come from an evaluation by each teacher/supervisor of what they consider to be the essential basics given the fact that most groupworkers eventually work unsupervised and also given that fact that time in the learning situation usually dictates that the essentials are all that might be acquired. This basic level of acceptable performance should be clearly identified by teachers/supervisors – it forms the foundation for later development and if it is not properly laid down causes endless problems at all later stages.

Complexity

Learning to understand group behaviour is a never-ending task and at this level of approach is therefore an extraordinarily complex procedure. The actual skills of groupwork founded upon this understanding are fundamentally simple. One of the great problems for learners is that they transfer the complexity of one into a complicating of the other.

Groups are collections of individuals

There is always some element of conflict between the claims of the individual and those of the group of which he/she is part. A group works when neither claim swamps the other. There are no guidelines to judge when this occurs or should there be – other than that the level of commitment is appropriate to the group's stage of development.

Support systems

It has been evident for a long time now that all people working with others require some system from which they can derive support. In this sense support means some place and some persons in which and with whom ideas, frustrations and successes can be exchanged, and where there exists some level of understanding of what is involved. The cardinal destroyers of groupworkers as of others are neglect, under-appreciation and isolation from others similarly engaged. Network systems are an obvious answer but have an unenviable reputation of being extremely costly in terms of effort and energy to maintain.

Adaptability	Basic groupwork skills have been shown to be adaptable to cope with many kinds of personal handicap. What is needed in all circumstances is some clear understanding of how any handicap affects the way a person relates to others, for example, in forms of communication, and to adapt some leadership behaviours to use the ways the handicapped have adapted, to forge links for others in the group.
Credibility	Perhaps one of the foremost assets any teacher/supervisor should aim to possess is 'credibility'. Like trust, this is often based on the way people see behaviour as being competent, but it is also based on the spread of these perceptions to different generations of learners in what is best described as a 'reputation'. Credibility introduces an element of certainty into what can otherwise be a fairly unsure situation.
Consistency	There is some evidence (Maier 1967) that successful professional practice relates much more directly to purposefulness and 'internal consistency in the theoretical propositions' which are used than in the kind of theoretical concepts they are.
Methods	Hartford (1967) lists five methods: didactic and/or class discussion; case study; observation; simulated experience; and use of the class as a clinic for practice problems.

Strategies

1 Recognition of need

Perhaps one of the most salient points about adult learning – it implies that where people can be led to recognize, or in their own right decide, that in order to do something or to proceed further with something in which they are interested and concerned about, they need to learn to collect more information or acquire new skills, the learning process can be very rapid and very complete. The problem lies in exposing the need for recognition. Too often adult learners have to acquire the techniques of discovering their real needs before those needs can be met. This can only be done by helping each person to disclose, in their own terms, what it is they think they require and to examine with due care and attention the evidence which would indicate that they are actually on the right track. There is perhaps nothing quite so arrogant as the trainer who assumes without investigation exactly what it is his/her learners need to know. He/she may be absolutely right, but this in no way dissolves the arrogance. The most potent help he/she can give is to encourage and support a growth of insight into what is required; to develop private acceptance and a clear understanding of the gaps that need to be filled.

2 Clarification of role

From the point of view of the learner there is nearly always some confusion about what particular role a groupwork trainer/teacher is occupying at any particular instant.

There are several possible strategies for dealing with this:

(a) The trainer must make public his/her recognition that he/she occupies different roles. These must be explained and as far as possible defined and given boundaries, for instance, the powers and authority vested in each role and especially how and when they may be in conflict.
(b) When a role change occurs it must be signalled verbally and, in the early stages of a group, feedback obtained that the signal has been received and understood.
(c) There is a great need to deal with different responses to confidences which different roles are able to produce. It may be that the following ground rules should be made explicit:

  (i) As a person occupying different roles, for example, social worker or groupworker, there are different responses to confidential material.
  (ii) The different responses should be described and the appropriate responses defined, for example, as a groupworker information about abuse is something to be worked with in the group; as a social worker it may be something that has to be disclosed to others who may be legally or morally compelled to act upon it.
  (iii) It should be made clear that the leader will refuse to accept information of a particular kind without due warning of the possible consequences and of his/her obligation to act upon it.
  (iv) There must be a clearer realization that if having received this caution the information is still disclosed, it will be assumed that the consequences are accepted.

Example

A groupwork teacher on a social work course ran groups for students which were basically personal growth groups but were also part of the learning programme about groups. The course had an assessment system and within a very short space of time there was conflict between the groupwork teacher and colleagues on the basis that he possessed information about students, divulged in growth group sessions which might materially affect the assessment process if made generally available. The ground rules at the group sessions had specifically stated the probable connection between disclosure and assessment, but when such material became available to assessment panels, the groups became defensive and were eventually transformed into a kind of group that was much less devoted to personal growth.

The moral of this example reveals a clear dichotomy between the agreed rules and the expectations of group members. The latter had become sensitive to an accepting and enabling ethos within the group which manifestly overrules their rational understanding of the agreed rules.

3 Challenge

The simplest strategy which promotes effective and useful challenge to the power of the group leader(s) is quite simply based on the response a leader makes to challenge and which is observed by the group. Thus 'put-down' responses, 'ignoring', 'accepting as personal the challenge', all are potent demonstrations that, contrary to the leader's statement, his/her power is unassailable, or at least heavily defended.

Challenge to leadership is usually an indication that group members are beginning to exercise the responsibility for what the group does. It may under certain circumstances be a real conflict in that the leadership has proved to be woefully inept.

4 'Stuckness'

All groups appear to get 'stuck' at some time or another. Strategies here depend upon the assessed nature of the 'Stuckness':

(a) Is it a period of rest or consolidation? This is usually marked by the nature of the material discussed by the group which usually contains large elements of seeking to find common strands and underlying linkages in what they have been doing. There is also a relatively busy but contented atmosphere, and although there is no apparent movement forward there is a distinct sense that what is happening will decide in what direction and how the next forward movements will be made.

(b) Real 'stuckness' is patterned by confusion, an unhappy atmosphere, the group splitting into subgroups, some apathy, some anger and a sense of stagnation.

Having decided that 'real stuckness' exists, then action must be taken against it because it has a rather rapidly debilitating and destructive effect if not dealt with.

Thus the leader must assume responsibility for presenting to the group what he/she sees as happening. If this is accepted then the next stage must be to create a group review which is an active consideration of the path the group has covered, and if possible discover why it feels that it has arrived at an impasse.

Of course there is always the possibility that the 'impasse' may be absolute in the sense that constraints have imposed a block or blocks upon any progress which may have happened because the group was badly designed in not foreseeing this possibility, or circumstances have changed dramatically since its inception.

In either case the group must be assisted to look at the consequences of the situation and to consider the possibilities of action to effect positive change.

What emerges from this and many other strategies considered here is that the major obstruction to effective action in almost every case is the lack of any clear understanding of what is really happening. The ability to verbalize perceptions, to make them visible for others to contribute to and consider, is the single most important group skill in dealing with problems.

5 Termination

It is a truism that the moment of creation is the first moment of demise, but it is seldom clearly recognized that most groups are eventually designed to work themselves out of existence. Thus the primary strategy is to build the expectation of termination into the group design right from the beginning, whether this be individual termination or that of the group as a unit. It is also possible to prepare for termination, not so much as an end, but as a transition from one state to another, a process which is common enough in everyday life.

It has always seemed to me that groups which have a tremendous grief problem at termination have been ill prepared for what is essentially what they formed the group to achieve.

B Problems presented by and concerned with those in the student/ learner/apprentice role

Definition and comment

Once again this is a complex of problems relating to the student setting out to learn a 'new' set of skills based upon some 'new' knowledge. Groupwork has unfortunately acquired a reputation of being a difficult set of skills to learn, that is, the learning process or the methods of instruction are difficult, not to say painful, if rumour is to be believed. The degree of involvement of other human beings which is necessary both in learning and in practice implies a degree of closeness and thus exposure which has greater power to cause trepidation in the uninformed as they approach the process of learning about groups.

Examples of problems

A large number of problems presented by people in this area are basically 'fears' and in that sense they are not always specifically tied to entering, or being in, groupwork training:

'Will I be accepted by the group?'

'Will I get along with the group?'

'Will I be the odd one out?'

'Will I get involved?'

'I don't know what to expect.'

'Will I get out of the course what I most need?'

'Will I be able to take it all in?'

'I fear there will be too much theory and not enough practice, too many big words, too much writing of notes.'

'I fear a lack of openness within this group will inhibit learning.'

'I feel bad time-keeping by some will result in much time lost for all.'

'I am not quite sure how I will apply the skills I do learn.'

'I wish we had a residential weekend to start to enable members to get to know one another and to break down barriers.'

Analysis of problems

The two points which emerge most clearly from the problems quoted are uncertainty, and the expected difficulties of the transfer of learning from the course situation to practice.

The uncertainty factor is common enough to most learning situations but I would hazard a guess that the reputation which training in working with groups has acquired right across the field may have added a new dimension. This is especially so when, as is so often the case, a large element of the learning is experiential in nature.

The second point, that of the transfer of learning of a skill-acquisition into the workplace, is also common and is primarily the main argument for supervised practice. But not supervision in the sense of discussion about some past event but supervision of the groupworker in the actual work situation, with immediate post-group feedback and even, with the help of modern technology, feedback during the group session itself.

Useful ideas

The simplicity of true understanding A long time ago I was told that, no matter how complex an idea was, if I really understood it I should be able to explain it to an 8-year-old without difficulty. It often seems that some of the difficulties learners have with the complexity of group dynamics lies in the lack of an ability in teacher/supervisors to express those ideas simply enough.

Hooks

New learning has to be 'hooked' into pre-existing knowledge – and to make sense in those terms. It is just as important to build bridges between prior and new learning as to present the new learning well.

Transfer of learning

The translation of ideas into action has always posed many problems. There seems to be a qualitative gap between the understanding of ideas as ideas and the understanding of ideas as forming the bases of possible action. In fact I have grown accustomed to group-workers saying 'Yes I understand that [about some particular idea] but I don't know or can't see, what to do with it'. The answer, of course, is that there should be supervised practice of the actual translation process which should take at least two stages: (1) an examination of the ideas and an attempt to redraft them in situational terms; and (2) a practical attempt to use the redrafted ideas in an actual situation (see next section, Strategies, under the heading of 'Translation').

Strategies

There are four learning strategies of benefit to all those starting to learn about working with groups listed by Getzel *et al.* (1987) which will be briefly offered here:

1 The groupwork log

This is in essence a diary listing work and comments on it. It is not adequate just to record events; thinking, experiences, struggles, problems, and so on, should also be included. There is the perennial problem of trust if this log is to be used as a learning instrument in that it will need to be read by the tutor/supervisor. There is no easy path round this dilemma.

2 Group analysis

Essentially this requires that each student groupworker should 'look systematically at a group in a way that will aid their present understanding as well as guide future action'. It helps if some form of guidelines is available.

3 Record of service

The student should identify an ability or a problem (group or individual) occurring within a group with which they are working and analyse their own practice in relation to it in teı ns of:

(a) the problem;
(b) summary of work undertaken;
(c) systematic examination of (b);
(d) plans for future work;
(e) list the ideas found useful.

4 Approach to practice

Make as complete a statement as possible of his/her own practice, methods, style and techniques, theory, and so on.

That these strategies have been listed under the category devoted to learners rather than that devoted to teachers where it would be equally applicable is no accident. It is based upon the fact that groupwork learners have to be both learner and teacher in the lack of any other form of instruction. These simple strategies constitute the basis for self-learning as much as they do for external instruction, but they do require a degree of conscious discipline which is not easily or often come by.

Translation

The process of taking ideas, in this case basic research data on group behaviour, and translating them into strategies, goes like this:

A Research ideas (Feldman 1967)

1 Functional integration and interpersonal integration are strongly correlated at the individual level.
2 There is a low correlation between normative integration and functional integration.

B Translation

1 Functional integration = members co-operating and combining to achieve group goals, member harmony and to maintain good relationships with each other. Interpersonal integration = the degree of acceptance of members as measured by liking for each other.

 Thus the statement of research findings at (1) can be translated as – group members perform key group functions more effectively and willingly when they like and are liked by their peers.

2 Normative integration = consensus on group rules.

The second statement then translates as – obeying group rules has no direct connection with liking or being liked and also that the effective performance of key group tasks by group members is not necessarily related to sticking to the group's rules.

Strategy based on translation   It should be said here that a strategy may as well be based on an understanding of the negative consequences of doing something as of the positive.

Positive – an individual's liking for his/her peers and theirs for him/her can be produced by the groupworker indicating, but preferably demonstrating, that the individual possesses resources which are of recognized value to the group, for example:

> The integration of one group member was assured when the group leader was able to indicate that the member possessed skills in the design of computer software which would enable the group to overcome a major obstacle to efficient functioning, namely a multidisciplinary records system.

Negative – coercing a member into conforming to group rules is not very likely to make him/her more group task efficient or – clarifying group rules for a member is not especially effective in promoting reciprocal liking between that member and his/her peers. Schwartz (1976) said of this particular situation:

> A theory of practice is a theory of action, and action is not deducible from either knowledge or intention alone. If we knew everything there is to know, we would still have to decide what to do; and if our purposes were impeccable, the action based on them would still not be self-evident.

DISCUSSION

The points that emerge clearly in this chapter are the fascinating similarity of the roles of teacher/supervisor and of student/learner to those of group leader and group member and yet the problems are presented as belonging not to groupwork *per se* but to the education and training process.

There is less stress on a problem which was common just a short while ago which related to the supervision of groupwork learners by those who had little or no training in groupwork themselves and but little integrated and analysed group experience. There has always been the advantage in this kind of situation of the detachment of the supervisor from the commitment of the groupworker – an advantage which can and should be exploited to present a relatively unbiased response to what is happening in a group. I have used this situation many times in groups when a new member has been the focus of attempts by members to explain what it is they are doing and how. The lack of precise experience of the group makes the new member an invaluable asset in testing the quality of the clarity of members' understanding of what they themselves are doing or more accurately what they believe themselves to be doing.

I believe that to have been a member of a group on several occasions and to have experienced the anxiety of entry and the process of gradual integration makes more readily for an understanding of the fears and anxieties of learners in groupwork. Somehow the rumours which have circulated about some forms of groupwork training, and which have spread to cover all forms, have generated an increased anxiety in most first-time entrants into groupwork learning, and are realistically represented by those recorded here. A problem in itself, of course, but also a manifestation of the fact that though groups can and do create a mini-society with explicit rules of behaviour, they are, with only extreme exceptions, not the totality of their members' existence. The leakage across group boundaries in most directions which is quite immense, and in particular the 'baggage' that members bring with them into the beginning group experience, require very careful consideration. Once again it is essential that due consideration should be given to the world of experience of others and to the realization that verbal explanations are interpreted in the light of that experience.

Much care given in this area will pay big dividends later in the way new group members will approach their work. There is so much evidence that practitioners in the early days of exercising their skills use the methods by which they were taught as the basis of their new practice.

SECTIONAL REFERENCES

A Trainers, supervisors and teachers

Abels, P.A. (1970) 'On the nature of supervision: the medium is the group', *Child Welfare* 49(6): 304–11.

Atherton, J. S. (1986) *Professional Supervision in Group Care*, London, Tavistock Publications.

Davies, E. (1973) 'The use of T-groups in training social workers', *British Journal of Social Work* 3(1): 65–78.

Feldman, R. A. (1967) 'Determinants and objectives of social groupwork intervention', in J. L. Roney (ed.) *Social Work Practice*, New York, Columbia University Press.

Garvin, C. D. (1981) *Contemporary Groupwork*, Englewood Cliffs, NJ, Prentice-Hall.

Getzel, G. S., Kurland, R. and Salmon, R. (1987) 'Teaching and learning the practice of social groupwork: four curriculum tools', in Lassner *et al.* (eds) *Social Groupwork: Competence and Values in Practice*, New York, The Haworth Press, Chapter 3.

Golden, I. (1966) 'Teaching a model of groupwork skill: a field instructor's report', *Journal of Education for Social Work* 2(2): 30–9.

Hartford, M. E. (1967) 'The preparation of social workers to practice with people in groups', *Journal of Education for Social Work* 3(2): 49–60.

Katz, S. I. and Schwebel, A. I. (1976) 'The transfer of laboratory training: some issues explored', *Small Group Behavior* 7(3): 271–86, London, Sage Publications.

Maier, H. W. (1967) 'Application of psychological and sociological theory to teaching social work with the group', *Journal of Education for Social Work* 3(1): 29–40.

Miller, F. D. (1976) 'The problem of transfer of training in learning groups: group cohesion as an end in itself'. *Small Group Behavior* 7(2): 221–36, London, Sage Publications.

Rose, S. D. and Finn, J. (1980) 'Video tape–laboratory approach to group work training for undergraduates', *Social Work with Groups* 3(1), New York, The Haworth Press.

Sales, E. and Navarre, E. (1970) *Individual and Group Supervision in Field Instruction*, Michigan, School of Social Work.

Schwartz, W. (1976) 'Between client and system: the mediating function', in R. Roberts and H. Northen (eds) *Theories of Social Work with Groups*, New York, Columbia University Press, 182.

Viccaro, T. J. (1978) 'Social work practice with groups: a laboratory programme for the beginning undergraduate student', *Social Work with Groups* 1(2): 195–206, New York, The Haworth Press.

B Students/learners

Cohen, A. I. (1973) 'Group therapy: an effective method of self supervision', *Small Group Behavior* 4(1): 69–80, London, Sage Publications.

Mackey, R. A. and O'Brien, B. A. (1979) 'The use of diaries with experiential groups', *Social Work with Groups* 2(2): 175–80, New York, The Haworth Press.

O'Connor, G. (1979) 'Human relations labs as a required part of social work education and training', *Social Work with Groups* 2(1): 55–66, New York, The Haworth Press.

Oxley, G. B., Wilson, S., Anderson, J. and Wong, S. G. (1979) 'Peer-led groups in graduate education', *Social Work with Groups* 2(1): 67–76, New York, The Haworth Press.

Waldman, E. (1980) 'Co-leadership as a method of training: a student point of view', *Social Work with Groups* 3(1): 51–6, New York, The Haworth Press.

Part III

Discussion

Discussion

Chapter 8

Summing up

SOME REITERATION OF METHODS OF USING THIS HANDBOOK

It cannot be stressed too firmly that what has been presented here is essentially a method of dealing with the common problems which groupworkers and team leaders encounter in their daily practice. The method can be stated very baldly in that it requires a careful analysis of what it is that is presenting as a problem in order to clarify it from as many points of view as possible; then to select from the wide range of available information what seems to fit the clarified assessment; then to devise a method of proceeding based upon this and the specific knowledge of the situation; then to monitor the effects and to reassess in the light of any feedback and/or observation as necessary.

What is so clearly missing from so simplistic a statement are two factors:

1 The level of understanding each groupworker has of the 'tramlines' along which he or she operates and which therefore dictate to a considerable degree the way that he/she interprets or records group events, either successes or failures, and the
2 The degree of actual skill that the individual groupworker has for deriving a strategy, a scheme of action, from it and of being able to put it into place. In some ways the element of control of one's individual behaviour patterns which is required in order to be able to do this successfully is often regarded as something alien especially to those who implicitly believe that honesty and sincerity are consonant with uncontrolled or 'natural' behaviour. Suffice it to say at this point that the conscious use of skill, knowledge and understanding for the purpose of enabling others carries greater connotations of honesty and sincerity in my book than does the so-called natural response.

It is quite startling to see how little material there is in the groupwork literature which takes specific difficulties experienced by groupworkers, analyses the fundamentals of the problem, and suggests a clear method of procedure based upon a sound understanding of the dynamics involved (see Feldman (1969) for just such a presentation of a procedure).

OTHER STRATEGIES AVAILABLE FOR PROBLEM RESOLUTION AND MANAGEMENT

As will no doubt have been noticed on many occasions, the strategy of choice has been one which involved the sharing of responsibility for dealing with the problem with other members of the group. In fact all strategies tend to indicate the necessity at some stage for such sharing to take place. Leaders do have special responsibilities but members have responsibilities also, and there is no more effective way of indicating to a group where the power lies in the system than to exclude members from participation in, and discussion of, those matters which affect and concern them quite deeply. In fact, one of the most difficult changes that has to come about, before a groupworker becomes proficient in his/her professional role, is one which concerns just this matter of responsibility. In some cases, and in all cases at some times, direct, straight through responsibility taken by the leader is not only appropriate but necessary. At others the enabling process is essential – an indirect kind of responsibility which has as its objectives the nurturing of others in taking responsibility for themselves. The high visibility of leaders in any form of group makes it almost certain that their behaviour patterns will be the single most important source of information about their 'real' intentions for group and team members, whatever the leader's expressed intentions may be.

The other major contribution here must be based in the fact that all the resources available to the group are not just those which are contained within it. Such is the involvement of group members in some situations that there is no great possibility that the clarification, which is such an essential precursor stage in the process of coping with problems, can actually take place. When this situation occurs then the uninvolved outsider may be the best option. It is often said that the bystander sees most of the game. A comment which, while possessing a large element of undoubted truth, ignores the subtle and the not so subtle differences in the perception of bystanders.

There are probably two main categories of the uninvolved outsider, both can be of help to the beleaguered group. One is the person, who, while not possessing any great expertise in the matter of groups and group behaviour, is yet wholly untainted by the circumstances in which the group has its existence – in a word – an untrammelled commentator with no particular axe to grind as far as the group is concerned.

The second is the so-called 'expert' with wide and varied experiences of many different kinds of groups and their problems, whose main contribution lies in having seen something similar before and in knowing how various strategies to cope with the situation actually worked out in practice.

The fundamental factors of both kinds of uninvolved outsider help are first their distance from the constraining circumstances of the group and its situation, and secondly, what is seen by the group as their credibility.

There is an example given in this book of the distance a new member entering an established group may well possess. What was lacking in this instance was a recognition by the group that the new member possessed any credibility until this was made visible to the group by an outside helper who possessed great credibility. Most group members tend to see new entrants to their group, not as sources of possible help with clarification arising out of the need to be instructed in the ways of the group, but as lacking the shared experience of the established group members and thus not really understanding what is and was involved.

This is a classic case of how it is possible to turn what appears to be a liability into a useful asset, but it does require a change of attitude from the norm to work, and such a change is seldom possible without outside help.

WHAT HAPPENS WHEN STRATEGIES DO NOT WORK?

It is just as important, maybe even more important, to know when a strategy has not worked as to know when it has, and moreover, to know why. There are many reasons why a strategy may not work ranging all the way from the fact that it was the wrong one based upon a faulty or incorrect assessment of what was required, through the implementation of a good well-founded strategy at the wrong time and/or inappropriately located, to the fact that the situation for which the strategy was designed has changed either in itself or from the addition or deletion of some principal elements.

The problem is how to be able to decide what went wrong. To help in this quest I give a check list below which should enable a groupworker to be systematic in the search for causes:

1 There must be something to check – so there needs to be a baseline against which change can be measured.
2 There must be clarity – are you sure what went wrong? If not try to spell out what you think may be the issues involved.
3 Why do you think that it went wrong? This is very difficult for a large number of reasons, so careful scrutiny is essential:

   (a) The most obvious connections between cause and effect are often as wrong as they are right because they are based upon wrong assumptions.
   (b) The most important way to counteract this is to get opinions from as many people who are involved as possible – the more ideas that you get the wider the search will be and some apparently highly improbable connections may begin to show a much closer causal connection and linkage.

Example

In my experience there are three most commonly advanced causes of the failure of a group strategy:

(a) Lack of skill on the part of the leader(s).
(b) Uncompromising, difficult or obstructive group members.
(c) Impossibly restricted constraints imposed upon the group – physical, organizational and programmatic.

More subtle but equally powerful influences such as timing, inadequate data, inaccurate assessment and a host of other internal and external factors are seldom rated at their true value. It is quite common that where a group leader feels a considerable degree of responsibility for his/her group, either because it is necessary or because he/she has not been able, or perhaps has no intention of, sharing that responsibility with the group members, the primary response to strategy failure is self-blame.

Major pressures like responsibility predispose such responses and there is a great need to be much more objective in the search for causes. The end result may well confirm the original impression, but that will now have a much surer grounding.

The most dangerous possibility for the group is that wrong or faulty assessment of the cause of strategy failure will lead to the implementation of curative strategies which, because they are based in a wrong diagnosis, have the potential to make matters worse by adding to the original problem, which in any case will continue to exist.

(c) To involve the group in a discussion about what went wrong is an obvious ploy, but the effects of using it must be given careful consideration along several parameters:

   (i)   Whether the members of the group have such security needs that the kind of exposure could be seriously threatening.
   (ii) Is the group at a stage of development where such a procedure could well exacerbate already existing vulnerabilities, for example, during an internal power struggle?
   (iii) Are the group leaders prepared and able to accept the kind of response they may well get from the group?

Finally, in any consideration of what went wrong there is the basic need to take advantage of mistakes to adapt and to learn. But the mere fact of admitting a strategy failure and of pronouncing an intention of not repeating the error is a pointless exercise if there is still no understanding on a rational and realistic basis of how it happened in the first instance.

SUMMING UP

It must be reasonably obvious to any groupworker or team leader who has looked even cursorily at the problems listed here that they are familiar. I referred to this point in the introduction and speculated that the reiteration of the same or similar problems by successive generations of groupworkers might be due to the lack of an adequate apprenticeship form of training. I have found myself asking the question 'Why don't people learn?' and also saying, 'These are the same kind of problems that everybody else has got!', so many times that I feel that I must return to the matter here.

Over the years one thing has become fixed in my mind which is the extreme reluctance groupworkers seem to show about the whole process of sharing experience and knowledge. They operate groups which have a democratic/ sharing base, but the idea of sharing their problems or successes, their skill attempts and their burgeoning understanding seems to be imbued with a sticky reluctance even under some degree of coercion and support.

When questioned about this there is a response almost certainly containing a large element of blame for lack of time, or of opportunity. When the logic of this is pointed out, that is, that the consequences of not making time available to consult, to share, to read, to talk is most probably that of the stagnation of skill development and thus the provision of a poorer service than might be possible, and also entails a clear reduction in the level of job satisfaction, this is acknow- ledged to be true. But this somewhat grudging admission is usually accom- panied by a statement to the effect that there is little that can be done about it.

Of course this is not true. The allocation of time in any professional role has many determining factors, but one of the most important is the individual professional's priority system. This means that hard choices have to be made and there is the necessity of understanding the system in which each profes- sional works well enough to make a reasonable disposition of priorities, for example, one which is neither so contrary as to create a constant state of conflict and an exorbitant and costly diversion of energies away from the pro- fessional task, nor so accommodating that the task and its performance are dictated wholly by the system which is itself founded on perhaps a very dif- ferent set of priorities.

'Why don't people learn?' may then be answered, not only by the acknow- ledged fact that learning situations are not only difficult to achieve in current circumstances, but also that learning may be the personal and individual respon- sibility of the groupworker and thus requires the commitment of energy to set in motion what is required.

Alternatively, groupwork may represent such a small proportion of the daily workload that such a commitment would be excessive. It is clear that there is still only a small interest in groupwork as a method of working with people amongst the managers of organizations, which may well account to a con- siderable degree for the lack of regard for their work which not only permeates through to groupworkers but also significantly affects their performance.

Lest this seems to be unduly negative, I must record the fact that it has been my privilege to work with many people whose enthusiasm and energy devoted to improving their groupwork knowledge and skills for the benefits that this will bring to those with whom they work, has been a joy to observe. I hope they, and anyone else who might be interested, can gain some little relief from the impasse created by the lack of training opportunities and managerial disregard from this handbook.

REFERENCES

Feldman, R. A. (1969) 'Group integration: intense interpersonal dislike and social groupwork intervention', *Social Work* 14(3): 30–9.

Index

abilities 49–51
ability 48, 168
accelerators 9
access 132
acceptance, private 88–9
acknowledgement 42–3
activity groups 119
actor/observer effect 12
administration 114–15
age difference 29-30
agreement *see* contract
aims (goals) 12, 27, 28, 43–4, 54–64;
    leadership 27, 158–62; multiplicity of
    158–9
Altman, I. 29
apathetic people 3, 29, 38, 41
apprenticeship 5, 16, 173–7, 187
appropriateness 134
approval, gestures of 20
arrestive approach 18
assessment 103, 166, 167, 169
assessor, external 108, *see also* outsider
attendance problems 65, 72–3, *see also*
    continuity, dropping out
attention 105
attitudes 37–40, 130
attraction, interpersonal 30
avoidance 65

backgrounds, different 29–30
baseline, establishment of 103, 106–7
behaviour: consequences of 50, 80,
    91–2; disruptive *see* disruption;
    effect of 92; individual patterns 183;
    'natural' 144, 183; of group
    members 64–76; patterns 38;
    protective 39
behavioural exposure 124

Blake, R.R. 70
blaming others 66, 73, 75
Blau, P.M. 114
blind spots 156
Bradford, L.P. 3, 6

Carter, L.F. 107
challenge 66, 168, 172
change 11–12; in groupwork 16;
    measurement of 103–9, 185; of goals
    57; subgroup effect 95
claims, group/individual 168, 169
clarification 21; of goals 57, 60–1;
    of role 171–2; of strategy failure 185
clarity, personal 160
class 48–9
cliques 95
closed groups 10, 69, 96–9, 126
cognitive dissonance 40
cohesion 30
collusion 93
commitment 49, 56–7, 96, 126, *see also*
    motivation
communication 116; ability 161;
    consensual 21; effect of group size 132;
    strategies 117
complexity 169, 175
concern for people/task 70
confidences, keeping 65
confirmation 21
conflict 3, 36, 66, 67, 148–53; blindness
    71; resolution/management 70–1
conformity 88–9
consensual: communication 21; core 89
consensus 12, 56, 61–3, 86, 132
consequence: experience of 50, 80, 91;
    positive/negative 177;
    system communication 116

consistency 170
content 105–6
continuity 65, 129
contract 58–9, 86, 88, 95, 161
controlling behaviour 43, 44
coping strategy 4, 75
cost/reward 31, 56
countervailing approach 19
co-working 154
credibility 170

decision-making: constraints on 116; inadequate 3; task 157–8
Dentler, R.A. 152
dependency 65, 66
depressed people 41–2
description 21
design of group 132–8
development see group development
developmental: patterns 125; sequences 11, 155
diary, groupwork 175, see also record keeping
Diedrich, R.C. 90, 157
difference 8, 30–3; acceptance of 63–4
directive: behaviour 18–19; groups 18, 70; style 153–4, 158
dis-approval, gestures of 20
discussion 21, 92
dislike 15, 75
disruption (disruptive behaviour) 12, 14–15, 65–7, 77, 81, 145, 148–53
diversity see difference
dominant personalities 32, 38, 42–3, 65
Douglas, T. 70, 130, 135
dropping out 46, 65, 67, 97, see also attendance, continuity dyadic relationships 92
Dye, H.A. 90, 157

elderly people 119
El-Shamy, S. 126
enabler 167
energy: levels 42; positive 31, 36–7; resources 148
enhancing approach 18
environmental constraints 120, 162, see also settings
equality, exercise of 45
Erikson, K.T. 152
esteem 54, see also value
ethnic minorities 8

ethos 120
evaluation 103–4, 108
exhortation 21
expectation 49, 56, 61, 120, 172, see also aims
expertise 36
experts 184
explanation 21
exposing 21
expression 21
expression of understanding 21
expulsion 88, 90, 151, see also removal

facilitative style 70, 158
facilitator 165, 167
fatigue 167, 168
feature analysis theory 11
feedback 17, 45, 95, 106–7, 116, 161
Feldman, R. A. 142, 176, 183
fight see conflict
filter 59–60
fish-bowl exercise 96
flow charts 6
Frey, D.E. 71

game-playing activities 46
Garland, J.A. 74
Garvin, C.D. 96, 107
Gershenfeld, M.K. 153, 156–7
gestures 20
Getzel, G.S. 175
goals see aims
Gordon, T. 157
ground rules 80, 86, 88, 89–90, 171–2
group: as system 25, 85–109; conditions 27, 112–13; created 85; design 41, 132–8; development 4, 25, 31, 98, 122, 155; dynamics 9, 41, 141; functioning 66; goal facilitation 107; identity 146; life 12; life time 126; maintenance 5, 6, 74, 75; measurement of change 27, 85, 103–9, 185; nature of problems 10–14; needs 168, 169; normative structure 27, 85, 86–92; open/closed 10, 27, 85, 96–9; operating conditions 25; organization 113–18; preparation for 15; processes 9; role structure 27, 78, 85, 99–103, 155–6; settings 118–22, 162; size 128–32; sociability 108; starting/stopping 10; strategy failure 185–6; 'stuck' 172–3; subgroup structure 27, 85, 92–6; successful

135–6; termination 10, 97, 103, 145, 168, 173; time factor 122–8; turnover of members 65; unique nature of 4
group analysis 175
group behaviour theory 8
group leaders: behaviour 141; emergence of 131; responsibility felt by 12–13, 186; roles 102–3, 165, 166–7; suspicion-enhancing behaviours 44; trust-enhancing behaviours 44-5; *see also* leadership
group members 80–1; abilities 27, 28, 46–54; aims 27, 28, 43–4, 54–64; as components 9; biographical characteristics 27, 28, 29–37; contact time 126; deviant 95; dislike among 15; disruptive 12, 14–15, 77, 146; diversity 8, 30–3; dominating 32, 38, 42–3, 65; new 50–1, 88, 146, 184–5; performance and behaviour 27, 28, 64–76; personality and attitude 27, 28, 37–46; problems 25, 28–81; roles 27, 28, 76–80; selection 30, 33–4, 40, 59–60; timid 147–8
'groupthink' 9
groupwork, complexity of task 160
groupwork log 175, *see also* record keeping
groupworkers: experienced 5; potential ability 168–9; replacement 162–3; selection 167; training 165–78
Gruen, W. 36–7
guidance 130

handicap, physical 167, 168
Hare, A.P. 130, 131
Hartford, M.E. 42, 170
hearing impairment 167
Henry, M. 98
hidden agendas 39, 57
hiding 130
Hodge, J. 135
holding 49, 67, 81, 124
Hollander, E.P. 152
honesty 45, 87, 183
hooks 175
Horwitz, M. 3, 6

ideas 130
image projection 78
independence 153
individual prominence 107

induction groups 119
information: presentation 117; quality 33–4, 81, 108–9, 116, 136
integration: functional 176; interpersonal 176; normative 177
interdependence 134
interstices 115–16
intervention skills 142, 145–6
interview, pre-group 58
isolated people 29, 41
isolation, reduction of 96

Jones, E.E. 22

knowledge: level of 134–5, 140, 141–4; practice 143–4; theory 142–3
Kolodny, R.L. 74

Lang, N. 157, 158
leadership: aims 27, 158–62; behaviour 141; challenge to 172; continuum 160; definition 156; energy 36–7; knowledge 27, 140, 141–4; operations 18–19; performance 27, 153–8; process 25; shared 155; skills 27, 140, 144–53; style 153–8; *see also* group leaders
learning group 165
learning, transfer of 175
listening 46, 48, 49
log, groupwork 175, *see also* record keeping

McGrath, J. 29
Maier, H.W. 170
maintaining approach 18
maintenance, group 5, 6, 74, 75
management 117
measurement (of change) 103–9; forms of 107–8
memory 106
methods, groupwork teaching 170
modelling 45, 80, 91–2
modifying approach 19
moralizing 45
Moreton, J.S. 70
motivation 39, 146, *see also* commitment

Napier, R.N. 153, 156–7
'natural' behaviour 144, 183
nature 93–4
needs, group/individual 168, 169; recognition of 170–1

network systems 169
newcomers 50–1, 88, 146, 184–5
Nisbet, R.E. 22
non-participation 3, 68
normative structure 86–92
norms 87–8
number in group 128–132

objective, being 46, 49
observation 104–5, 108
observer/actor bias 12
observers 4
open groups 10, 67, 96–9
operational policy 57
originating ideas 93
outsider, uninvolved 184, *see also*
    assessor, external

pairing 94, 95, 131
participation 68
patterns 106; developmental 125; in
    groups 122; recognition 10–12
persistence of disruption 152
personal: aims 43–4; growth 34, 171–2
personality difficulties 37
planning 132–5
Polyani, M. 108
positive energy 31, 36–7
power 66–7, 161; social 155; struggles 65,
    66, 68–9
practice: approach to 176; knowledge
    143–4
prejudice 68, 75
preparation 132, 135
presentation 117, 168
Preston-Shoot, M. 107
priorities 117
prison 135
probation work 119, 121
problems: analysis of 16–17; classification
    system 26–7; common 7–10; focus of
    14–15; identification of 13–14, 25–6;
    source material 6–7; unique nature of 4
process 105–6
programme adjustment 96

rating scales 107
reality strategy 43–4, 121
reassignment 80, 102
recapitulation 157
record-keeping 10–11, 16, 106–7, 126–7,
    176

reductive approach 18
reflecting 21
regularities 4
reinforcement 80, 102
relationships: dyadic 92; interpersonal
    130–1; structure of 155–6; to task 130;
    with teacher/supervisor 5, 168
removal from group 43, 75, 151, *see also*
    expulsion
renegotiation of goals 57
repetition 12
research: ideas 176; material 142–3
resources 46–7, 48, 51–2, 117
responsibility: group leader's feelings
    12–13, 186; issues 65, 71–2, 75
revealing 21
reviewing procedures 157
rewards 31, 56, 72, *see also* satisfaction
role: analysis 79–80; changes of 168, 171;
    clarification of 171–2; consequence 80;
    demonstration 78–80; entrapment 78;
    leadership 140, 153–4, 166; model 96;
    modelling 21; performance 77–8; play
    75; structure 35, 78, 99–103, 155–6;
    trainer 166, 171; understanding of 13;
    watch-dog 80
rules 87, *see also* ground rules

Sabath, G. 153
sanctions 88, 90–1
satisfaction 39, 56, 131, 160
scale and proportion 123–4
scapegoating 65–6, 67–8, 73–6, 77, 168
scene, total 161
Schwartz, W. 177
Scott, W.R. 114
security 49
selection: of group members 30, 33–4, 40,
    59–60; of groupworkers 167; theories
    of 30
self-awareness 156, 160
self-esteem 48, 68, 147–8
self-help groups 8
Self Report 107
sequence of events 11
sessional duration 125–6
settings 118–22
sex difference 29
shared leadership 155
sharing 12, 187
signalling 168
silences 13, 145

similarity 12
simplicity of understanding 174–5
size of group 128–32; optimum 132
skill (groupwork): acquisition 174;
    development of 5, 16–17; leadership 27,
    140, 144–53; transfer of new 174
Smith, D. 94
social: groupings 29–30; power 38, 155
spacing of sessions 125–6
status 31, 46–7, 48, 53–4, 152–3
Stock, D. 3, 6
strategies: failure of 185–6; nature and use
    18–22; sources 7
structure 31; normative 86–92; of
    relationships 155–6; role 35, 78,
    99–103, 155–6; subgroup 27, 85, 92–6;
    task 34–5
'stuck' group 167, 168, 172–3
student problems 173–7
style, leadership 140, 153–8
subgroups: formation 93; identification
    94–5; relationships between 131;
    structure 92–6
subjective impressions 16
supervision, problems of 25, 165–78
supervisors 166–73
support systems 114, 169
suspicion 44–6
system: decisions 117; group as 25,
    85–109; group within 116–18; playing
    115; thinking 115

tacit knowing 108
task: group formation 96;
    structure 34–5
teachers 166–73

team, multi-disciplinary 9, 13
termination of group 10, 97, 103, 145,
    168, 173
threat 132
time: constraint 127–8, 157–8; factor 9,
    31, 81, 122–8, 136; management 125,
    187
timidity 147–8
tolerance 45
total scene 161
training 25, 165–78; student problems
    173–7; trainer problems 166–73
training courses 8
transfer of learning 175
transformation 10
translation 176–7
trust 31, 39, 45–6, 87, 124; lack of 37, 38,
    44

understanding: level of 183; simplicity of
    174–5

value, individual 31, 35–6, 47, *see also*
    esteem
victim: professional 77; selection of 74;
    see also scapegoating
video recording 118, 145
visibility 130, 156, 161
volunteers 64, 100, 154

watch-dog role 80
Window, J.-H. 156
withdrawal 66, 86
words, forms of 20–1, 145
working group 126
worth 31, 35–6, 47